Breakthrough Japanese

Breakthrough Japanese

20 MINI LESSONS FOR BETTER CONVERSATION

Hitomi Hirayama

KODANSHA INTERNATIONAL
Tokyo • New York • London

Distributed in the United States by Kodansha America, Inc., and in the United Kingdom and continental Europe by Kodansha Europe Ltd.

Published by Kodansha International Ltd., 17–14 Otowa 1-chome, Bunkyo-ku, Tokyo 112-8652, and Kodansha America, Inc.

The ideographic kanji illustrations on pp. 77–78, 105–106, and 109–110 are based on illustrations by Noriko Matsui that appear in *Shimomura-shiki shōgaku kanji gakushū jiten* by Noboru Shimomura (Tokyo: Kaisei-sha, 1987).

ISBN 4–7700–2873–3
First edition, 2004
10 09 08 07 06 05 04   10 9 8 7 6 5 4 3 2 1

www.kodansha-intl.com

CONTENTS

PREFACE

A foreign friend had asked me the difference between the phrases "shitsureshimasu" and "sumimasen." I had no idea what to tell her, and this was an awakening to me. Although I was Japanese and spoke Japanese every day of my life, I had no idea how to teach someone else how to use the language. This was the beginning of my interest in Japanese.

That was more than twenty years ago. Since that time I have been exploring the question of how to teach Japanese to non-native speakers in an accessible, enjoyable way.

In the language school that I run in Tokyo and where I have taught Japanese to businesspeople, diplomats, and others for many years now, my approach focuses on what I call "natural Japanese." The emphasis is not on outlining one grammatical concept after another, but on using the language in an enjoyable way. My teaching materials are filled with quizzes and games and other activities. I include grammar explanations, of course, but only where they are really necessary.

Those class materials gave birth first to a language column in the *Daily Yomiuri* newspaper called "Pera Pera Penguin's 5-minute Japanese Class," and then to this book. *Breakthrough Japanese* collects and amplifies some of the best of those columns.

To language teachers I would point out that I have not targeted learners of a single skill level here. Lessons are built around topics and should be interesting to beginning, intermediate, and advanced learners. When using this book, the teacher's role should not be to explain so much as to navigate. I find that this approach is easy and fun for learners and teachers alike.

To learners I would give this advice: when studying Japanese, you may sometimes have trouble understanding why Japanese say something in a particular way. Seeking the cultural difference that would explain things, however, can sometimes create a barrier between yourself and the language. The important thing, I would say, is to keep your mind neutral, to leave the door open between yourself and the language. Be open to not understanding everything, and to letting the language gradually become a part of you.

"Why a penguin?" you may ask, looking at the illustrations in this book. The habitat of the penguin is vast, spanning several continents. To me the penguin is a fitting symbol of a creature that lives beyond borders. When we set out to learn a new language, we should be like penguins: global creatures!

A Note About Pronunciation and Romanization

The pronunciation of vowels in Japanese is as in Italian or Spanish. When Japanese is written in roman letters, a macron (straight horizontal line) is placed over certain vowels; this indicates that a particular vowel should be doubled—elongated—as in the English words "aah" or "ooh." Another mark to notice is the double consonant: double t, s, p, k, sh, or ch. The double consonant in these words represents a syllabic stop (a necessary pause between consonants), as in the English word "bookkeeper."

Words from foreign languages, like "hot dog" or "classical (music)," are written in this book in English in italic type, rather than being spelled out phonetically in katakana, the Japanese script used for foreign loan words. This is done to save students having to spend time learning the "Japanese" pronunciation of foreign words. Learners should simply pronounce these words as in English, but slowly.

Finally, sentences in the text are given in a three-line format: in English, in Japanese script, and in romanized letters. Below the romanized line, in smaller type, are definitions of the more difficult vocabulary in the sentence. In some cases, certain words in the romanized line may be underlined; this shows that those words together form a single phrase, as in "o-mie desu," which is then defined below as "has arrived (honorific form)."

Acknowledgements

This book came about over the course of several years, and many people helped make it possible.

Fifteen years ago, Mr. Jaemes Shanley, recognizing that I had a mountain of valuable teaching material, gave me my first Mac and encouraged me to set up a language school.

Mimi Oka-san, my best friend, was the voice behind the penguin in this book that asks the all-important questions about Japanese at the beginning of each lesson. Thinking long and hard about Japanese from the point of view of the learner, Oka-san was able to provide me with invaluable insights that eventually became material for this book.

I am grateful to Atsushi Kodera-san at the *Daily Yomiuri*. Kodera-san was the first in the publishing business to take me seriously. Thanks to the *Daily Yomiuri*, which admittedly took a risk in choosing to publish my work, students around the world have come to enjoy my lessons.

For the illustrations, I thank Masako Ban-san and Yuko Matsushima-san. Ban-san, who drew the penguins and designed the original lessons, has been a good friend over the years. The lessons in this book took shape, in part, because of her intuitive understanding of my approach and her ability to translate my ideas into a charming and practical design.

Yasuhiro Koga-san translated some of the lessons in this book, and for his help I am very grateful. Mr. Paul Hulbert helped in an editorial capacity at various stages. Thank you, Paul.

Elizabeth Floyd, my editor in New York, and Michael Staley, my editor at Kodansha International in Tokyo, were extremely patient with me, and I feel very lucky to have been able to work with them. For that matter, I would like to thank both Kodansha International and Kodansha America.

Sachiko Konami-san, also in New York, encouraged and supported me throughout the writing of this book, and I thank her, too.

Kaoru Ueda-san and Minako Nishizawa-san ran Japanese Lunch, my language school, for months while I was writing this book, which surely would not have seen the light of day without their resilience; I thank them as well as every other teacher at Japanese Lunch.

Finally, I would like to thank my mother Yaeko and my dog Ohayo for their emotional support and their good-natured tolerance of all the time I devoted to this project. My mother will no doubt be the happiest person in the world to see this book finally published. Ohayo, meanwhile, will be glad to get back to her schedule of regular morning walks.

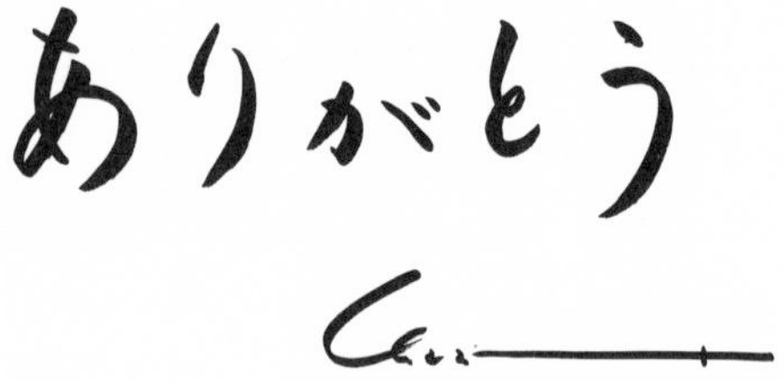

Pole-**san**
Pole-**sama** Po-**chan**

Mr. Pole

I get called so many different things: Pole-**san**, Pole-**sama**, even Po-**chan**. I'm confused. **san** doesn't seem to be used in just the same way as "Mr." or "Ms.," even though my dictionary says it is. And another thing: I always thought Japanese people put their family name before their given name. But I've noticed that they reverse this order when writing their name in Roman letters.

You're right: **san** and Mr. or Ms. aren't really identical. In Japan people are addressed in different ways according to relationship or situation. And to answer your second question: Most people today reverse their names when writing in Roman letters to make them easier for non-Japanese to understand. Recently there are also a few who want to maintain the traditional order of family name first as a matter of national identity and pride.

Hirayama

san is a respectful way to address or refer to other people

さん

When speaking to Japanese people (even in English), it is best to use san after either their given name or family name. Japanese people often feel uncomfortable if their names are used without san.

鈴木さん　ゆき子さん

Ms. Yukiko Suzuki ➡ Suzuki-san or Yukiko-san

(given name) (family name) → (family name) (given name)

In business conversations san (or the more polite sama) can also be added after the name of a client company.

東京証券 ➡ 東京証券さん／様

Tokyo shōken (Tokyo Securities) ➡ Tokyo shōken-san/-sama

Sometimes san shouldn't be used. When speaking to a third person, don't refer to members of your own group (yourself, your family, your company, your colleagues) using san.

■ introducing a coworker to a client

This is Ms. Suzuki.

鈴木です。

Suzuki desu.

Suzuki-san!

■ introducing a member of your family to a friend

This is my wife, Amy.

妻のエイミーです。

tsuma no *Amy* desu.

my wife

様

sama is very polite, and is used mainly to address customers. It is also used in writing.

addressing friends/acquaintances

When addressing one another, childhood and old school friends usually use given names or nicknames (often a shortened version of the name) followed by chan or kun. (chan is normally used when addressing children, and kun male children.) Those who meet as adults, however, usually use family names.

addressing:	female	male
child*	given name + chan	given name + kun or chan
adult**	family name + san	

* or childhood friend, school buddy, or close friend
** acquaintance or friend whom you have met as an adult

PRACTICE

Fill in each of the blanks below with san, sama or — (= "nothing").

■ at the front desk of a hotel

Receptionist: (to a guest)
Mr. Oda, Mr. Miki is waiting for you in the lobby.
尾田 ______、三木 ______ がロビーでお待ちでございます。
Oda ___❶___, Miki ___❷___ ga *lobby* de
o-machi degozaimasu.
waiting (honorific form)

■ talking to a company receptionist

Inoue: My name is Inoue, I'm from Shibuya Bank ...
渋谷銀行の井上 ______ ですが、
Shibuya ginkō no Inoue ___❸___ desu ga,
bank

I have an appointment to see Mr. Yokota at 9 o'clock.
9時に横田 ______ とお約束しています。
ku-ji ni Yokota ___❹___ to o-yakusoku shite imasu.
9 o'clock — have an appointment (honorific form)

Receptionist: (dialing Mr. Yokota's extension)
Mr. Yokota! Mr. Inoue from Shibuya Bank is here.

横田 ______！ 渋谷銀行の井上 ______ がお見えです。

Yokota __❺__！ Shibuya ginkō no Inoue __❻__ ga o-mie desu.
has arrived (honorific form)

■ **at a hospital**

Nurse: (to a patient)
Mr. Taro Fujita! Please come into (exam room) 5!

藤田太郎 ______！ 5番にお入りください。

Fujita Taro __❼__ ! go-ban ni o-hairi kudasai.
number 5 come in (honorific form)

■ **at a bank**

Teller: (calling the next customer to the counter)
Japanese Lunch Co., Ltd.

ジャパニーズランチ株式会社 ______。

Japanese Lunch kabushiki-gaisha __❽__.
Co., Ltd.

■ **at a restaurant**

Hayashi: My name is Hayashi, I have a reservation for 7 o'clock.

7時に予約をした林 ______ です。

shichi-ji ni yoyaku o shita Hayashi __❾__ desu.
7 o'clock made a reservation

Waitress: Mr. Hayashi. Please come right this way.

林 ______、どうぞこちらに。

Hayashi __❿__, dōzo kochira ni.
please this way

answers ❶ sama ❷ sama ❸ — ❹ san/sama ❺ san ❻ sama
❼ san ❽ sama ❾ — ❿ sama

a few more courtesy titles

shi 氏 is a written form, used in the media in place of **san**.

> 高田氏
> Takada-shi
> Mr./Ms. Takada

dono 殿 is an old form. It is less respectful than **sama**. Nowadays, it is rarely used except in certain official documents.

> 高田殿
> Takada-dono
> Mr./Ms. Takada

onchū 御中 is a written form, used instead of **sama** when addressing a letter to a company or organization, rather than to an individual.

> 渋谷区役所御中
> Shibuya kuyakusho onchū
> Shibuya Ward Office

Pole-**dono**.
(**dono** is used often in samurai movies.)

TALK

Try to introduce yourself and talk about your family.

1. Introduce yourself:

Good morning	/	Hello	/	Good evening
おはようございます		こんにちは		こんばんは
ohayō gozaimasu		konnichiwa		kombanwa

My name is _______.

Say your name just the way you would say it in your own country. Speak slowly so the person can catch your name.

_______ です。

_______ desu.

Please call me _______ nickname .

_______ と呼んで下さい。

_______ to yonde kudasai.
please call me

I'm from _______ country .

_______ から来ました。

_______ kara kimashita.
from came

I like _______ and _______ hobbies or things you like .

_______ と _______ が好きです。

_______ to _______ ga suki desu.
like

[Please have a good relationship with me.]

どうぞ宜しくお願いします。

dōzo yoroshiku o-negai shimasu.

(This phrase is often used in Japanese when first meeting or when starting out working together. It means roughly, "I am looking forward to knowing you/working with you.")

II. Talk about your family:

There are ______ `number of people` people in my family.

______ 家族です。

______ kazoku desu.
family

(When counting the people in your family, you must count yourself as one! So you, one brother, one sister and your two parents would be five, not four.)

1 person	2 people	3 people	4 people	5 people
1人／一人	2人／二人	3人／三人	4人／四人	5人／五人
hitori	futari	san-nin	yo-nin	go-nin

There are ______ `number of people` of us [brothers/sisters].

______ きょうだいです。

______ kyōdai desu.
siblings

(When counting the siblings in your family, count yourself as one! So you, your brother, and your sister would be **san-nin kyōdai.**)

I have a younger sister and an older brother.

妹と兄がいます。

imōto to ani ga imasu.

younger sister	older sister	younger brother	older brother
妹	姉	弟	兄
imōto	ane	otōto	ani

NOTE: Use these terms only to refer to your own brothers/sisters.

III. Talk about your children:

I have _______ number kid(s).

子供が _______ います。

kodomo ga _______ imasu.
kids

I have _______ number daughter(s) and _______ son(s).

娘 _______ と息子 _______ です。

musume _______ to musuko _______ desu.
daugter son

My daughter/son _______ name is _______ years old.

娘／息子の _______ は _______ です。

musume/musuko no _______ wa _______ desu.

counting ages

1 year old	2 years old	3 years old	4 years old	5 years old
1歳	2歳	3歳	4歳	5歳
is-sai	ni-sai	san-sai	yon-sai	go-sai

6 years old	7 years old	8 years old	9 years old	10 years old
6歳	7歳	8歳	9歳	10歳
roku-sai	nana-sai	has-sai	kyū-sai	jus-sai

11 years old	20 years old	21 years old	30 years old	40 years old
11歳	20歳	21歳	30歳	40歳
jūis-sai	hatachi	nijūis-sai	sanjus-sai	yonjus-sai

anata = "you"?

Mr. Pole

I thought **anata** meant "you," but I'm confused. I went to a friend's house for dinner the other night and his mother kept saying to me, **anata wa nani o nomimasu ka**? ("What will you have to drink?") and **anata wa niku ga ii desu ka? soretomo sakana ga ii desu ka**? ("Do you like meat? Do you like fish?") I figured **anata** means "you," so eventually I called her **anata**, too, but when I did she looked offended.

Hirayama

anata is not a direct equivalent of "you." Used mainly toward equals or junior colleagues, it can cause offense if used in the wrong situations. (In olden days **anata** was used toward people of higher rank and denoted respect, but this is no longer the case.) All in all, it's safest to simply avoid using **anata**, and instead call people by their family name or given name, plus **san**.

using anata inappropriately can cause offense

あなた

If you know a person's name, it is best to use their family name or given name, plus san, when addressing them. Many people are offended if called anata by someone who knows their name.

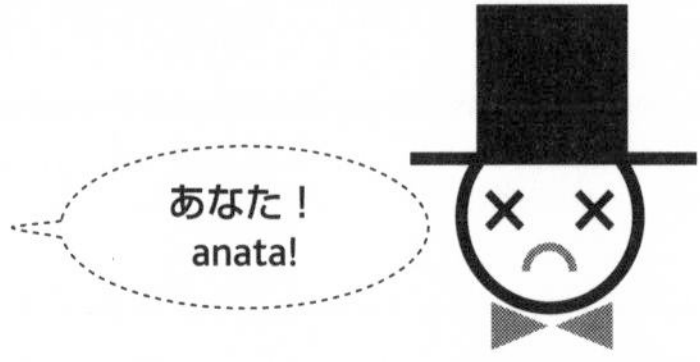

Use anata like the English "you" only if you don't know the person's name.

PRACTICE

Fill in the blanks with the appropriate Japanese expression (anata or person's name + san).

■ at a conference

Speaker: Japan is in a recession. How about your country?

日本は不景気ですが、______ の国はどうですか？

Nihon wa fukēki desu ga, __❶__ no kuni wa dō desu ka?
(Japan / recession / but / country / how?)

■ on the street

Police officer: Is this your car?

この車は ______ のですか？

kono kuruma wa __❷__ no desu ka?
(this / car)

You're parked in a no-parking zone.

ここは駐車禁止ですよ。

koko wa chūsha-kinshi desu yo.
(here / no parking / I tell you)

■ **to a friend**

Mr. Pole: How are you?

お元気ですか。

o-genki desu ka.
well

Friend: I'm fine, thank you. And you?

はい、おかげさまで。_______は？

hai, okagesama de. __❸__ wa?
set phrase: thankfully/I'm happy to say …

---

answers ❶ anata ❷ anata ❸ *Pole*-san

distinguishing "my group" from "others"

Japanese speakers view people as belonging to particular groups. At the most basic level in any conversation there are two groups:

MY GROUP:		OTHERS:	
	myself		somebody else
	my family		somebody else's family
	my colleagues		somebody else's colleagues

Apart from a few specialized cases, Japanese people do not use possessive pronouns (my = watashi no or your = anata no) to describe members of a family group. Instead, they use one set of expressions for members of their own group and different expressions for members of another group.

This is my wife.

~~私の~~ 妻です。

~~watashi no~~ tsuma desu.
my wife

Is this your wife?

~~あなたの~~ 奥さんですか?

~~anata no~~ okusan desu ka?
your wife

I. terms used for husbands and wives

There are many terms for husbands and wives. Below are the basic ones used for one's own spouse.

	husband	wife
in public (to outsiders)	主人 shujin	妻 tsuma, 家内 kanai (young men don't use kanai much)
casual situations (with friends)	うちの人 uchi no hito, だんな danna (young women use danna; can sound uncouth)	うちの uchi no, うちのやつ uchi no yatsu (sounds uncouth), よめさん yomesan (sounds uncouth)

NOTE: Often spouses leave out names altogether and just say ね ne ("hey") or ちょっと chotto ("you know …") to get the other's attention.

II. terms used for family members

Here are a few examples of the words used to describe family relationships. Remembering these can help avoid confusion.

	my group	others
father	父 chichi	お父さん otōsan
mother	母 haha	お母さん okāsan
husband	主人 shujin	ご主人 go-shujin
wife	妻 tsuma	奥さん okusan
child	子供 kodomo	お子さん okosan
brothers & sisters	きょうだい kyōdai	ごきょうだい go-kyōdai
parents	両親 ryōshin	ご両親 go-ryōshin
family	家族 kazoku	ご家族 go-kazoku

PRACTICE

Fill in the blanks with the appropriate Japanese term for the situation.

■ **to a friend**

Mr. Pole: Are you going to the party tomorrow night?

あしたの飲み会どうしますか？

ashita no nomikai dō shimasu ka?
tomorrow drinking party how about

Friend: It's up to you.

______ 次第ですよ。

___❶___ shidai desu yo.
up to

■ **to a friend**

Mr. Pole: How are your parents doing?

______ はお元気ですか？

___❷___ wa o-genki desu ka?
healthy

Friend: They're fine. Thanks for asking.

ええ、おかげさまで。

ē, okagesama de.
set phrase: thankfully/I'm happy to say …

■ **to a friend**

Mr. Pole: How many are there in your family?

______ は何人ですか？

___❸___ wa nan-nin desu ka?
how many

Friend: There are five of us.

______ は5人です。

___❹___ wa go-nin desu.
five people

■ **to a friend**

Mr. Pole: How old are your children?

______ はおいくつですか？

___❺___ wa o-ikutsu desu ka?
how old? (honorific form)

Friend: The older is five, and the younger is three years old.

上が5歳で、下が3歳です。

ue ga go-sai de, shita ga san-sai desu.
oldest youngest

■ **at a job interview**

Interviewer: Would the next person please come in?

次の方どうぞ。

tsugi no kata dōzo.
next person please come in

Person next to you: You're next!

___❻___ の番ですよ。

______ no ban desu yo.
turn I tell you

answers ❶ *Pole*-san ❷ go-ryōshin ❸ go-kazoku ❹ kazoku
❺ okosan ❻ anata

TALK

How would you say these phrases in Japanese?

❼ (casual style)
Oh, this is difficult ...
❽ (casual style)
I've got no time! I've got to hurry!
❾ (casual style)
Ah ... I'm tired ...
❿ (casual style)
I'm finally done!

answers

❶ 山口です。
Yamaguchi desu.

❷ 山口です。
Yamaguchi desu.

❸ エイミー・クーパーです。
Amy Cooper desu.

❹ きょうはありがとうございました。
kyō wa arigatō gozaimashita.

❺ 失礼します。
shitsurē shimasu.

❻ どうぞ。
dōzo.

❼ ううん、難しいなあ。
ūn, muzukashii nā.

❽ 時間がない！急がなくちゃ！
jikan ga nai! isoganakucha!

❾ ああ、疲れた。
ā, tsukareta.

❿ やっと終わった！
yatto owatta!

like and dislike

One of our executives, Mr. Oda, asked me last week how the new young woman in our office was working out. I answered **suki desu** ("I like her"). Mr. Oda raised his eyebrows, as if I had said something strange. What was wrong with my answer?

Most Japanese textbooks and dictionaries translate **suki** as "like." But when used about people, **suki** is actually closer in meaning to the English word "love." So be careful when using **suki** or **suki desu**—you might suggest you are in love with someone.

Hirayama

expressing liking with ii and suki

いい

Use ii to praise or admire something:

I like this coffee cup.
このコーヒーカップいいですね。
kono *coffee cup* ii desu ne.

好き

Use suki to say that you like something very much:

I like classical music.
クラシックが好きです。
classic ga suki desu.

to talk about love

愛しています aishite imasu is a literal translation of "I love you, " but Japanese people rarely use the phrase in real life. If you want to say that you love someone or something very much, it's better to say 大好きです daisuki desu.

expressing dislike with kirai and chotto …

DIRECT kirai きらい

INDIRECT amari suki ja nai desu あまり好きじゃないです
not like

OR

chotto … ちょっと…

kirai is strong and very direct, so it is usually avoided. It's better to use more vague and indirect expressions, as below.

Friend: Do you like Japanese food?
日本の食べ物は好きですか？
Nihon no tabemono wa suki desu ka?
food

Pole-san: I'm not that crazy about it …
あまり好きじゃないです…
amari suki ja nai desu …
not like

chotto is the most indirect, or polite, way to refuse something gently, without actually saying that you don't like the thing being offered.

■ **at a restaurant**

Friend: Shall we order this dish?
この料理を注文しましょうか。
kono ryōri o chūmon shimashō ka.
order shall we?

Pole-san: I'm not so crazy about spicy food [salty food] …
辛いもの［しょっぱいもの］はちょっと…
karaimono [shoppaimono] wa chotto …
spicy/hot things

PRACTICE

Fill in the blanks with the appropriate Japanese expression for the English "like" or "dislike": ii, suki, kirai, or chotto.

■ at a seafood restaurant

Mr. Pole: I like this restaurant. (This restaurant is nice.)

このレストラン ______ ですね。

kono *restaurant* ___❶___ desu ne.
isn't it?

Mr. Oda: What are your "likes and dislikes"? (Is there anything in particular you like or don't like?)

何か好き嫌いありますか？

nanika suki-kirai arimasu ka?
anything likes & dislikes do you have?

Mr. Pole: Hmmm … I really like sashimi.

そうですね…刺身が特に ______ です。

sō desu ne … sashimi ga tokuni ___❷___ desu.
well … especially

But I don't like squid so much …

でもイカは ______…

demo ika wa ___❸___ …
but squid

■ while eating

Mr. Oda: Oh, by the way, how is the new person in your office?

ところで、新しいスタッフはどうですか？

tokorode, atarashii *staff* wa dō desu ka?
by the way new staff member how is?

Mr. Pole: I like him. (He's a nice person.)

______ 人です。

___❹___ hito desu.
person

answers ❶ ii ❷ suki ❸ chotto ❹ ii

the kanji for suki

好

kō: favorable, good
su(ki), -zu(ki), kono(mi): like, fond of

Combining "woman" (女 onna) and "child" (子 ko), this kanji originally meant "young woman" or "girl." Because young females were considered "beautiful" or "desirable," this kanji came to mean "like" or "good." Related words that use this same kanji include:

likes and dislikes	好き嫌い	suki-kirai
free choice; to each his own	好き好き	suki-zuki
taste, preference	好み	konomi
good reputation, acclaim	好評	kōhyō
ideal, best	絶好	zekkō

PRACTICE

Fill in the blanks below with the correct phrase from the list of words above containing the kanji 好.

❶ I have no particular likes or dislikes.

_______ は特にありません。

_______ wa tokuni arimasen.
in particular have no

❷ Today is a perfect (ideal) day for golf, isn't it?

きょうは _______ のゴルフ日和ですね。

kyō wa _______ no *golf*-biyori desu ne.
today / perfect day for golf

Many Japanese businessmen like to practice their golf swing in train stations and other places.

❸ My wife's taste is very particular (finicky, exacting).

妻の _______ は難しいです。

tsuma no _______ wa muzukashii desu.

particular (difficult)

❹ To each his own! (often used negatively)

_______ ですから。

_______ desu kara.

❺ That new product has a good reputation, doesn't it?

あの新製品は _______ ですね。

ano shinsēhin wa _______ desu ne.

that new product

answers ❶ suki-kirai ❷ zekkō ❸ konomi ❹ suki-zuki ❺ kōhyō

another set phrase using **suki**

unskillful but enthusiastic (crazy about something, but not good at it)

下手の横好き

heta no yoko-zuki

bad at

Excessive pride isn't appreciated in Japan. It is even best to be humble when one excels in something and receives praise for it. This set phrase can be used to show humility when praised.

Mr. Tada: You are good (at it).

上手ですね。

jōzu desu ne.

good at

Mr. Pole: Oh, no. I just enjoy it. I'm not any good at it.
いいえ、下手の横好きですよ。
iie, heta no yoko-zuki desu yo.

Mr. Tada: No, really! You are good!
いえ、本当に上手ですよ。
ie, hontō ni jōzu desu yo.
really / I tell you

Mr. Pole: Really? Thank you.
そうですか。ありがとうございます。
sō desu ka. arigatō gozaimasu.
really? / thank you

responding to praise

Mr. Tada: Your Japanese is good!
日本語、上手ですね！
Nihongo, jōzu desu ne!
good at (casual term)

Mr. Pole: No, I still have a long way to go.
いえ、まだまだです。
ie, mada mada desu.
not yet

OR

Oh no, not at all.
いえ、とんでもないです。
ie, tondemonai desu.
ridiculous

TALK

The following dialogue presents some handy phrases for interacting in a Japanese home. One phrase has been left blank. See if you can fill it in.

■ **at the front door**

Friend's mother: Please come in.

どうぞお入り下さい。

dōzo o-hairi kudasai.

come in (honorific form)

Pole-san: (says while entering)

お邪魔します。 OR 失礼します。

o-jama shimasu. shitsurē shimasu.

sorry to disturb you / excuse me

(These phrases are conventions used when entering somebody's home.)

This is a small present for you.

あのう、これどうぞ。

anō, kore dōzo.

Friend's mother: Oh, thank you.

あ、すいません。

a, suimasen.

(suimasen is a more friendly, casual pronunciation of sumimasen.)

■ **in the house**

Friend's mother: Please make yourself at home.

どうぞお楽に。

dōzo o-raku ni.

comfort

Pole-san: Thank you.

失礼します。

shitsurē shimasu.

失礼します。
shitsurē shimasu.

Friend's mother: Do you like tempura?

天ぷらお好きですか？

tempura o-suki desu ka.

like (honorific form)

Pole-san: Yes, I like it very much.

ええ、______.

ē, ❶______.

■ **when leaving**

Pole-san: Thank you very much for inviting me today/for everything.

きょうはありがとうございました。

kyō wa arigatō gozaimashita.

(This phrase can be used anytime you are about to say goodbye to someone who has just done you a favor or shown you kindness.)

Thank you for the wonderful meal.

ごちそうさまでした。

gochisōsama deshita.

(This phrase could be used in place of kyō wa arigatō gozaimashita above. It is used after eating a meal and expresses your appreciation for the food eaten.)

It was a lot of fun./I had a good time.

とても楽しかったです。

totemo tanoshikatta desu.

very was fun

---

answers ❶ daisuki desu

ごちそうさまでした。
gochisōsama deshita.

hai = "yes"?

Mr. Pole

I had promised to have dinner with my friend last night and called her at the office to decide what time to meet. When the receptionist answered I asked, **Ueda-san irasshaimasu ka** ("May I speak with Ms. Ueda?"). She replied, **hai, tadaima kaigi-chū desu ga ...** ("Yes, Ms. Ueda is in a meeting now, but ..."). She had said yes (**hai**), so I waited and waited, but my friend never did come on the phone. What's up with this word **hai** anyway?

---

hai, wakarimashita ("Yes, I see what you mean"). Japanese people like to use the word **hai** often in daily conversation. The English word "yes" is usually used as the direct opposite of "no," but **hai** is a much broader term and can have very different meanings in different situations—it can even mean "no."

Hirayama

the many uses of hai

はい

hai can mean all these things:

I understand.	OK!
I see.	Here!
Uh-huh.	Attention!
Certainly!	Yes. (That's right.)
Sure!	No. (That's right.)

It is used 1) to confirm one's presence;

■ **at a business conference, answering a roll call**

Organizer: Nishizawa-san.
西沢さん。
Nishizawa-san.

Participant: Here!
はい!
hai!

■ **on the phone**

Caller: Is this Ueda-san?
上田さんですか？
Ueda-san desu ka?

Ueda-san: Yes, this is she.
はい、上田です。
hai, Ueda desu.

2) to get somebody's attention;

■ just before the start of a meeting

Organizer: May I have your attention. It's time to start.

はい、それでは始めます。

hai, soredewa hajimemasu.

then will start

3) to show understanding;

Manager: Please come early tomorrow morning.

あしたの朝早く来てください。

ashita no asa hayaku kite kudasai.

morning early please come

Secretary: I'd like to, but I'm afraid I can't …

はい、でも…ちょっと難しいです。

hai, demo … chotto muzukashii desu.

but difficult (impossible)

4) to respond to a request, suggestion or invitation;

■ responding to a request

Manager: Could you do this, please?

これお願いします。

kore o-negai shimasu.

this please

Secretary: Certainly.

はい。

hai.

■ responding to a suggestion or command

Manager: It's getting late. Go on home now.

遅いのでもう帰りなさい。

osoi node mō kaerinasai.

late so soon go home (blunt form)

Secretary: Thank you, sir!

はい。

hai.

■ **responding to an invitation**

Manager: Let's have dinner tonight!

こんばん、食事でも？

komban, shokuji demo?

tonight meal or something

Secretary: Sure, that would be great.

はい、ぜひ。

hai, zehi.

by all means

5) to respond to a question with "yes";

Manager: Are you Japanese?

日本人ですか？

Nihonjin desu ka?

Employee: Yes, I am.

はい。

hai.

Manager: Is Mr. Inaba there?

稲場さん、いますか？

Inaba-san, imasu ka?

is there?

Employee: Yes, he is.

はい、います。

hai, imasu.

and 6) to respond to a question with "no";

Manager: Is Mr. Inaba not there?

稲場さん、いませんか？

Inaba-san, imasen ka?
isn't there?

Employee: Yes (that's right/I'm listening to you), he's not here.

はい、いません。

hai, imasen.

Colleague: Tomorrow aren't you going with us?

あした一緒に行きませんか？

ashita issho ni ikimasen ka?
together / aren't you going?

Pole-san: No, I can't.

はい、でもちょっと…。

hai, demo chotto ...
(soft refusal)

NOTE: Japanese people don't usually like to give a negative-sounding response right away, so they soften their answer by saying hai first, before giving the more negative-sounding answer, such as imasen.

PRACTICE

Fill in the blanks with either hai or iie (= "no"). Remember that hai is an all-purpose response and, as the examples above show us, can be used with negative as well as affirmative answers.

■ **on the phone**

Mr. Lee: Hello.

もしもし。

moshi moshi.
hello (used on the phone)

Receptionist: Hello. This is Japanese Lunch.

_______、ジャパニーズランチでございます。

___❶___, *Japanese Lunch* degozaimasu.
(humble form of desu)

Mr. Lee: This is Lee of KB TV. I'd like to talk to Ms. Ueda.

KBTVの李ですが、上田さんお願いします。

KBTV no *Lee* desu ga, Ueda-san o-negai shimasu.
(o-negai shimasu: please)

Receptionist: Certainly! Please hold on a minute.

_______、少々お待ちください。

___❷___, shōshō o-machi kudasai.
(shōshō: a little; o-machi kudasai: please wait (honorific form))

Hello? Sorry to have made you wait.

もしもし、お待たせいたしました。

moshi moshi, o-matase itashimashita.
(moshi moshi: hello; o-matase itashimashita: made you wait (humble form))

I'm afraid she is away from her desk right now.

ただ今席をはずしております。

tadaima seki o hazushite orimasu.
(tadaima: just now; seki o hazushite orimasu: seat/desk be away from (humble form))

Mr. Lee: I see, so she isn't there?

そうですか、いらっしゃいませんか。

sō desu ka, irasshaimasen ka.
(sō desu ka: I see; irasshaimasen ka: not there (honorific form))

Receptionist: That's right.

_______。

___❸___.

Mr. Lee: Do you know when she'll be back?

いつ頃戻られますか？

itsugoro modoraremasu ka?
(itsugoro: about when; modoraremasu: return (honorific form))

Receptionist: She is in the office, so she should be back soon.

社内におりますのですぐ戻ります。

shanai ni orimasu node sugu modorimasu.
be, exist (humble form)

Shall she call you when she gets back?

戻りましたらこちらからお電話いたしましょうか？

modorimashitara kochira kara o-denwa itashimashō ka?
when she gets back / from this side / call you (humble form)

Mr. Lee: No, I'll be going out soon so …

いいえ、すぐに出ますので…

iie, suguni demasu node …
soon / will leave / so

I will call her back later.

ではまた私から電話します。

dewa, mata watashi kara denwa shimasu.
again / from me / will call

Receptionist: I see. Thank you very much (that will be good).

______、ではよろしくお願いいたします。

__❹__, dewa yoroshiku o-negai itashimasu.
then / please (humble form)

Mr. Lee: Okay, goodbye!

______、失礼します。

__❺__, shitsurē shimasu.
goodbye (used on the phone)

answers ❶ hai ❷ hai ❸ hai ❹ hai ❺ hai

REVIEW

Pole-san is calling his friend Takashi Hayashi on the phone. Fill in the blanks with the appropriate form of the person's name (adding **san** or not).

Pole-san: Hello. Is this the Hayashi residence?

もしもし、＿＿＿＿のお宅ですか？

moshi moshi, ＿❶＿ no o-taku desu ka?
residence (polite form)

Obā-chan*: Huh?

え？

e?

*obā-chan (obā-san): "grandmother" (in this case, Takashi's)

Pole-san: Umm … My name is Pole.

あのう、＿＿＿＿と申しますが。

anō, ＿❷＿ to mōshimasu ga.
my name is (humble form)

Obā-chan: Huh? Who is this? I can't hear you …

え？ どちら様ですか？ ちょっと遠いんですが…

e? dochira-sama desu ka? chotto tōi'n desu ga …
who (polite form) far (=can't hear)

Pole-san: My name is Pole and I work in the same company as Takashi.

孝さんと同じ会社の＿＿＿＿です。

Takashi-san to onaji kaisha no ＿❸＿ desu.
same company

Obā-chan: Hm? Hole-san?

え？ ホールさん？

e? *Hole*-san?

Pole-san: Is Takashi there, please?

あのう、______ いらっしゃいますか？

anō, __❹__ irasshaimasu ka?
is there (honorific form)

Obā-chan: Huh? Ta? ka? shi? Just a minute.

え？ た？ か？ し？ ちょっと待ってね。 casual style

e? ta? ka? shi? chotto matte ne.
a little please wait

Takashi: This is Takashi. Who is this?

______ ですが、どちら様ですか？

__❺__ desu ga, dochira-sama desu ka?
who (polite form)

Pole-san: Hello! This is Pole.

こんばんは。______ です。

kombanwa. __❻__ desu.

Takashi: Oh, Pole-san? Sorry, sorry! My grandmother doesn't hear so well …

あ、ポールさん？ ごめんごめん、おばあちゃん耳が遠いので…

a, *Pole*-san? gomen gomen, obā-chan mimi ga tōi node …
sorry grandmother can't hear so well therefore

answers ❶ Hayashi-san ❷ *Pole* ❸ *Pole* ❹ Takashi-san ❺ Takashi ❻ *Pole*

kanji numerals

一 二 三 四 五 六 七 八 九 十

Mr. Pole

It seems like the prices of Japanese food on menus are always written in kanji numerals. Since I can only read 一, 二, and 三 (1, 2, and 3) I can only order things that are very inexpensive, like soba or o-nigiri (rice balls). I'd like to be able to eat other things, but I'm scared to order them if I can't read the price. I suppose I had better learn some more kanji numerals.

Yes, the prices of Japanese food on menus are usually written in kanji numerals, so it would be scary to not be able to read them. If you don't learn the price until you get the receipt, it is like **ato no matsuri** ("shutting the stable door after the horse is stolen"). I think you need to buckle down and learn the kanji for 4 through 10. Then you'll be able to order sushi, shabu-shabu, or whatever you like!

Japanese numbers: 1 through 10

Arabic numerals	kanji numerals	pronunciation of the numerals (see also p. 125)	pronunciation of numbers when counting objects
1	一	ichi	hitotsu
2	二	ni	futatsu
3	三	san	mittsu
4	四	shi/yon	yottsu
5	五	go	itsutsu
6	六	roku	muttsu
7	七	shichi/nana	nanatsu
8	八	hachi	yattsu
9	九	kyū/ku	kokonotsu
10	十	jū	tō

There is a fixed order for writing the different strokes in any Japanese kanji character. Below, the kanji are labeled with the order in which their strokes should be written. Trace over each kanji, following the instructions given for stroke order.

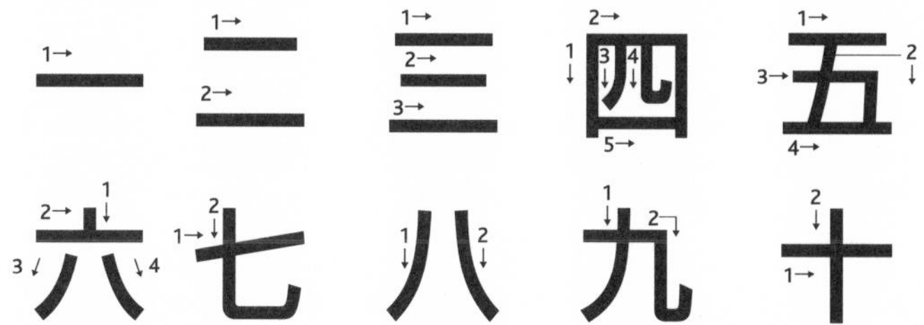

NOTE: the kanji for "zero" is O and is pronounced either zero or rē. Draw it as you would any other circle—there is no fixed stroke order for this number!

PRACTICE

I. kanji numerals

Fill in the boxes with the appropriate kanji numerals. (Kanji numerals are usually written vertically.)

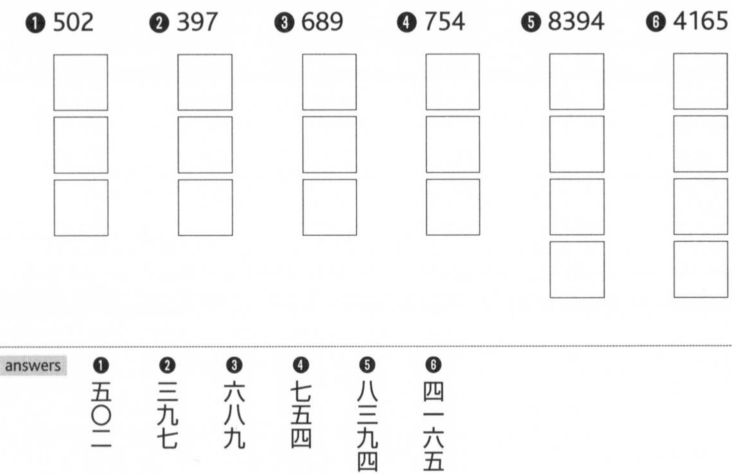

❶ 502
❷ 397
❸ 689
❹ 754
❺ 8394
❻ 4165
answers
❶ 五〇二
❷ 三九七
❸ 六八九
❹ 七五四
❺ 八三九四
❻ 四一六五

II. kanji numerals in male and female names

The following Japanese male names all end with the word 郎 rō (a common suffix used in men's names). Write the correct kanji numerals for the other syllables in the boxes. Refer to the pronunciation chart on the previous page as necessary.

The following Japanese female names all end with 子 ko (literally, "child"; a common suffix often used in women's names). Write the correct kanji numerals for the other syllables in the boxes. Refer to the pronunciation chart on the previous page, as well as p. 125.

❹ Yaeko □重子　❺ Fumiko □□子

❻ Minako □□子

answers ❶ 一郎 ❷ 五郎 ❸ 六郎 ❹ 八重子 ❺ 二三子 ❻ 三七子

III. kanji numerals in place names

Kanji numerals appear in many place names. Write the correct kanji numerals in the boxes. Refer to the pronunciation chart on p. 49, as well as p. 125.

❶ Shikoku □国

❷ Muikaichi □日市

❸ Mita □田

❹ Yotsuya □ッ谷

❺ Kujūkuri □□□里

❻ Shimantogawa □万□川

❼ Gotanda □反田

answers ❶ 四国 ❷ 六日市 ❸ 三田 ❹ 四ッ谷 ❺ 九十九里
❻ 四万十川 ❼ 五反田

IV. kanji numerals on menus

Write in the prices on the restaurant menu below.

寿司（sushi）	3500 円
そば（soba）	840 円
うどん（udon）	760 円
ビール（beer）	690 円
酒（sake）	940 円
ジュース（juice）	550 円

❶ 寿司 □□□□円
❷ そば □□□円
❸ うどん □□□円
❹ ビール □□□円
❺ 酒 □□□円
❻ ジュース □□□円

answers ❶ 三五〇〇 ❷ 八四〇 ❸ 七六〇 ❹ 六九〇 ❺ 九四〇 ❻ 五五〇

V. kanji numerals in idiomatic phrases

Here are six sayings that contain kanji numerals. The kanji numerals have been left for you to fill in. Write the correct kanji numerals in the boxes.

❶ a single, authoritative word

(Lit., “a single cry from the crane”)

❷ Rome was not built in a day.

ローマは［　］日にして成らず

Rome wa **ichi**-nichi ni shite narazu
day　not built (classical form)

❸ to round off numbers

［　］捨［　］入

shisha-**go**nyū
throw away　add to

(Lit., "four is down, five is up")

❹ to cooperate on a single task

［　］人［　］脚

ni-nin **san**-kyaku
people　legs

(Lit., "three-legged couple")

❺ someone whose resolve quickly dissipates

［　］日坊主

mikka bōzu
days　monk

(Lit., "three-day monk")

❻ to change again and again

［　］転［　］転する

ni-ten **san**-ten suru
change/turn/roll

(Lit., "changing twice, changing three times")

---

answers ❶ 鶴の一声　❷ ローマは**一**日にして成らず　❸ **四**捨**五**入
❹ 二人三脚　❺ 三日坊主　❻ 二転三転する

REVIEW

Now fill in the blanks with the appropriate saying from the preceding page.

❶ Please round up the numbers when you calculate.

_______ で計算してください。

_______ de kēsan shite kudasai.
with please calculate

9.6 → 10

❷ I get tired of things quickly and I don't stick with them.

_______ で長続きしません。

_______ de nagatsuzuki shimasen.
not keep at it

❸ Our negotiations will never end. They are always changing.

話し合いはなかなか終わらない。いつも _______.

hanashiai wa nakanaka owaranai. itsumo _______.
negotiations really do not end always

❹ We survived the crisis by pulling together and cooperating.

_______ で危機を乗り越えました。

_______ de kiki o norikoemashita.
crisis survived

❺ The company president has the last word, so we have to go back to the drawing board.

社長の _______ でやりなおしです。

shachō no _______ de yarinaoshi desu.
president do again

❻ Remember, Rome wasn't built in a day. Let's keep on trying!

_______ です。がんばりましょう。

_______ desu. gambarimashō.
hang in there

answers ❶ shisha-gonyū ❷ mikka bōzu ❸ ni-ten san-ten suru ❹ ni-nin san-kyaku ❺ tsuru no hito koe ❻ *Rome* wa ichi-nichi ni shite narazu

phrases involving numbers

Rice balls were given out to **each of the** homeless **people** (there).

ホームレスのひとりひとりにおにぎりが配られた。

homeless no **hitori-hitori** ni o-nigiri ga kubarareta.

to each one / rice ball / were passed out

I slept **all day** but I'm still tired.

一日中寝ていたのにまだ眠い。

ichinichijū nete ita noni mada nemui.

all day / slept / though still / sleepy

His teeth are all black because he smokes **from morning till night**.

四六時中タバコを吸っているので歯が黒くなった。

shirokujichū *tobacco* o sutte iru node ha ga kuroku natta.

all day (negative nuance) / smoking / teeth / became black

(shirokujichū literally means "four six hours throughout." The rather oblique meaning of this is "throughout four multiplied by six hours" = "throughout twenty-four hours.")

It's sad to be **all alone** on your birthday.

ひとりぼっちの誕生日は寂しい。

hitori-bocchi no tanjōbi wa sabishii.

all alone / birthday / lonely

It's fun to **live alone** and be able to do whatever you like.

一人暮らしの気ままな生活は楽しい。

hitori-gurashi no kimama na sēkatsu wa tanoshii.

living alone / as you like / lifestyle / fun

For a time there, I couldn't send any e-mail, which was not good at all.

一時的にメールが送れなくなって困った。

ichijiteki ni *mail* ga okurenaku natte komatta.

temporarily / couldn't send / was troubled

o or go?

I've learned that "flower" is **hana** in Japanese, and that family is **kazoku**, but I notice that Japanese often say **o-hana** or **go-kazoku**. How can I start using **o** and **go**, too? I don't know what words to attach **o** or **go** to. And what's the difference between them?

Both **o** and **go** are honorific prefixes. There are complicated rules about how to use them, and I will explain some of them here. Generally they are placed before nouns or adjectives, but certain words take **o**, and others **go**. Also, the rules are not fixed: one person may say **o-mizu** (water) and another person **mizu**. Generally women use honorifics more often, although both men and women use honorifics with clients and in other very polite situations. Interestingly, **o** and **go** usually do not attach to katakana words.

Hirayama

reasons to place **o** or **go** before a word

1) To make one's speech sound more polite or respectful
2) To beautify one's expressions
3) To soften language (mostly done by women)
4) To speak to children (with children, some people use **o** frequently)

o is for common words that are related to everyday life.

o + NOUN or ADJECTIVE

EXAMPLES:

NOUN	fish	魚 sakana	お魚 o-sakana
ADJECTIVE	well (fine, cheerful)	元気な genki na	お元気な o-genki na

ご

go is for words that denote an action or activity. (Generally, go is placed before kanji whose readings are of Chinese origin, but I think it is very difficult for students to distinguish which words these are. That's why I like to try to explain it this way.)

go + NOUN (especially a noun related to an abstract concept)

EXAMPLES:

introduction	紹介 shōkai	ご紹介 go-shōkai
contract	契約 kēyaku	ご契約 go-kēyaku

The chart on the following page shows a few examples of words that can take o and go. Of course, this is just the tip of the iceberg and there are many more words that are not on the list, so please make your own decisions by listening to the way that Japanese people around you use them. Attaching these prefixes to i-adjectives or na-adjectives is done mostly by older women, or toward customers.

	NOUNS		I-ADJECTIVES	NA-ADJECTIVES
o お	name お名前 o-namae	money お金 o-kane	busy お忙しい o-isogashii	well (fine, cheerful) お元気な o-genki na
	letter お手紙 o-tegami	sake お酒 o-sake		like お好きな o-suki na
	holiday お休み o-yasumi	telephone お電話 o-denwa	expensive お高い o-takai	be good at お上手な o-jōzu na
	medicine お薬 o-kusuri	work お仕事 o-shigoto	cheap お安い o-yasui	dislike お嫌いな o-kirai na
	soy sauce お醤油 o-shōyu	cold お風邪 o-kaze	fast, quick お早い o-hayai	quiet お静かな o-shizuka na
	chopsticks お箸 o-hashi	cooking お料理 o-ryōri	young お若い o-wakai	disappointing おいやな o-iya na
	talk お話 o-hanashi	rice お米 o-kome	hot お暑い o-atsui	sturdy, strong お丈夫な o-jōbu na
	drinks お飲み物 o-nomimono	shopping お買物 o-kaimono	cold (weather) お寒い o-samui	beautiful おきれいな o-kirē na
go ご	business ご用件 go-yōken	reservation ご予約 go-yoyaku	anxiety ご心配 go-shimpai	explanation ご説明 go-setsumē
	address ご住所 go-jūsho	departure ご出発 go-shuppatsu	order ご注文 go-chūmon	neighborhood ご近所 go-kinjo
	contact ご連絡 go-renraku	family ご家族 go-kazoku	confirmation ご確認 go-kakunin	message ご伝言 go-dengon

(white) commonly and generally used

(light gray) frequently and widely used

(dark gray) used mainly by older women, or toward customers

PRACTICE

Add o or go to any of the words in the following sentences, as necessary.

❶ Do you like sake?

酒は好きですか？

sake wa suki desu ka?

Yes, I do.

はい、好きです。

hai, suki desu.

❷ Thank you for calling. You seem to be pretty busy with work.

電話ありがとうございました。 仕事忙しそうですね。

denwa arigatō gozaimashita. shigoto isogashi-sō desu ne.

telephone thank you work seem busy

❸ How is everybody in your family?

家族の皆さん、元気ですか？

kazoku no minasan, genki desu ka?

family everyone well

They're all fine, thanks for asking.

はい、おかげさまで元気です。

hai, okagesama de genki desu.

set phrase: thankfully/I'm happy to say …

❹ Which Japanese food do you dislike?

日本の食べ物は何が嫌いですか？

Nihon no tabemono wa nani ga kirai desu ka?

food what dislike

❺ May I take your order?

注文は?

chūmon wa?
order

❻ So, you would like to make a reservation? Could you please give me your name, address, and telephone number?

予約ですね。名前と住所と電話番号お願いします。

yoyaku desu ne. namae to jūsho to denwa bangō o-negai shimasu.
reservation / name / address / telephone number / please

❼ Do you have time right now?

今、時間ありますか？

ima, jikan arimasu ka?
now / time / do you have?

---

answers

❶ o-sake wa o-suki desu ka.
hai, suki desu.

❷ o-denwa arigatō gozaimashita. o-shigoto o-isogashi-sō desu ne.

❸ go-kazoku no minasan o-genki desu ka.
hai, okagesama de genki desu.

❹ Nihon no tabemono wa nani ga o-kirai desu ka.

❺ go-chūmon wa?

❻ go-yoyaku desu ne. o-namae to go-jūsho to o-denwa bango o-negai shimasu.

❼ ima, o-jikan arimasu ka.

TALK

The following are some handy mealtime phrases. How many of them do you know?

I'm hungry.

おなかがすきました。

onaka ga sukimashita.
stomach / emptiness

It looks delicious, doesn't it?

おいしそうですね。

<u>oishi-sō</u> desu ne.
looks delicious

■ **before starting to eat**

It looks delicious, shall we start?

いただきます。

itadakimasu.

(There is really no good English translation for this phrase spoken just before eating.)

This is very delicious.

とてもおいしいですね。

totemo oishii desu ne.
very isn't it?

What is this?

これは何ですか？

kore wa nan desu ka?
this what

I'm full.

おなかがいっぱいです。

onaka ga ippai desu.
full

■ **after finishing a meal**

That was great. Thank you very much.

ごちそうさまでした。

gochisōsama deshita.

(Again, there is no exact equivalent of this phrase spoken after eating.)

It was delicious.

おいしかったです。

oishikatta desu.
was delicious

■ **at a sushi bar**

Waiter: Hello. How are you today? How many are you?

いらっしゃいませ。何名様ですか？

irasshaimase. nan-mē-sama desu ka?

welcome / how many people?

Customer: We are ______ people (see p. 19) . We'd like to sit at the counter.

______ です。カウンターお願いします。

______ people (see p. 19) desu. *counter* o-negai shimasu.

(Sitting at the counter at a sushi shop makes it easier to order since you don't need to know the names of all the fish. You can just point and say kore o-negai shimasu, "This one, please.")

Waiter: Have you decided what you would like?

ご注文は？

go-chūmon wa?

Customer: For now we'll have some beers.

とりあえずビールお願いします。

toriaezu *beer* o-negai shimasu.

for now

(toriaezu suggests that they need some more time before ordering their food.)

Waiter: (a few minutes later) Have you decided?

お決まりですか？

o-kimari desu ka?

decide (honorific form)

fish kanji

sakana (fish)

The kanji used to write the names of various fish may look so similar that they are hard to memorize, but actually there are reasons why each kanji is written the way it is.

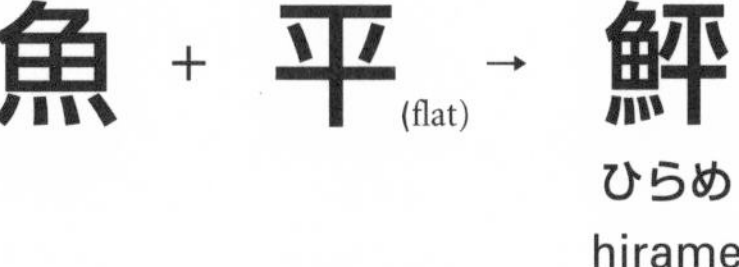

ひらめ
hirame
flatfish

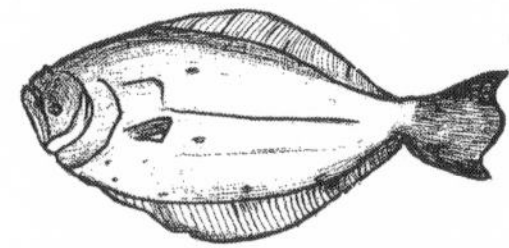

hirame has a flat shape.

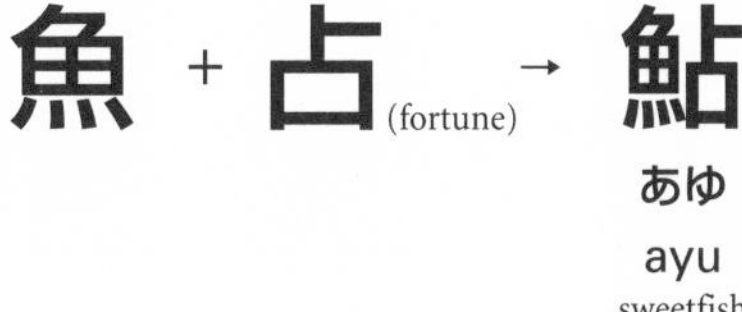

あゆ
ayu
sweetfish

In ancient times, **ayu** scales were used to tell fortunes.

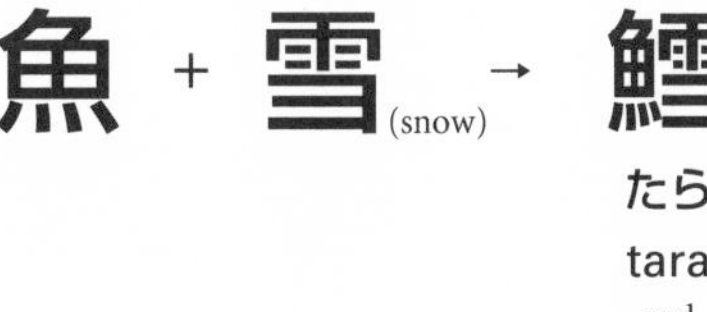

たら
tara
cod

tara is at its most delicious in winter.

さば
saba
horse mackerel

The **saba**'s body looks blue.

pocket phrases

I've been studying Japanese for a year now, but I'm still not any good at it. I don't seem to be able to have a real conversation. I have some friends who I could speak to in Japanese if I wanted, but I'm not sure how to go about trying to have an entire conversation.

This kind of frustration is common to people who are studying Japanese. I think it's the same for everyone. It takes a long time before your Japanese will start to sound really natural. Meanwhile, there is something you can do. No matter what your skill level, you can memorize the pocket phrases (phrases often used in conversation) in this chapter—without worrying about the grammar behind them—and start to use them as a way to improve the flow of your conversation in Japanese. First of all, though, we should look at several sentence-ending particles, since these are really basic.

Hirayama

forming a question

SENTENCE + か ka

ka functions like a question mark, with the difference being that ka is actually spoken as part of the sentence.

I think so.

そう思います。

sō omoimasu.

think

Do you think so?

そう思いますか？

sō omoimasu ka?

agreeing with someone, or seeking agreement/confirmation

SENTENCE + ね ne

It's hot today, isn't it.

きょう暑いですね。

kyō atsui desu ne.

hot isn't it

It sure is.

そうですね。

sō desu ne.

I agree

giving new information or advice

SENTENCE + よ yo

It's hard (you know)!

難しいですよ。

muzukashii desu yo.

I tell you

Oh, really?

え、本当？

e, hontō?

pocket phrases

I see.

そうですか。

sō desu ka. (intonation falls at the end of the sentence)

Is that so?

そうですか？

sō desu ka? (intonation rises at the end of the sentence)

I forgot.

忘れました。

wasuremashita.

I couldn't do it.

ダメでした。

dame deshita.

What's going to happen?

どうなりますか？

dō narimasu ka?
how become

We'll see (let's wait and see).

様子をみましょう。

yōsu o mimashō.
circumstances let's see

I hope so (I hope it's true).

そうだといいです（ね）。

sō da to ii desu (ne).
if it is, good

I hope not (I hope it's not true).

そうじゃないといいです(ね)。

sō ja nai to ii desu (ne).
if not good

Yes, so I heard.

そうらしいです。

sō rashii desu.
so it seems (they say)

(could you repeat it) one more time, please?

もう一度お願いします。

mō ichi-do o-negai shimasu.

Oh no (this is troubling).

困りました。 polite style OR **困ったな。** casual style

komarimashita. komattana.
troubles me (to bother one: komarimasu)

What's wrong? What's the matter?

どうしましたか?

dō shimashita ka?

What shall I/we do?

すいません、どうしたらいいですか?

suimasen, dō shitara ii desu ka?
how to do

I'm fine. (I'm all right.)

大丈夫です。

daijōbu desu.
all right

Don't worry about it.

心配しないでください。

shimpai shinaide kudasai.
worry please don't

Long time no see. It's been a long time.

お久しぶりです。

o-hisashiburi desu.

It's a small world.

世の中狭いですね。

yo no naka semai desu ne.
world narrow

I can't remember.

思い出せません。

omoidasemasen.
cannot remember (to remember: omoidashimasu)

Hang in there (keep at it/you can do it).

がんばって。 casual style OR がんばってください。 polite style

gambatte. gambatte kudasai.
try hard (to try hard: gambarimasu)

That was a great help/You saved me!

とても助かりました。

totemo tasukarimashita.
very helped/saved

(That's) too bad.

残念です（ね）。

zannen desu (ne).
a shame/pity

That sounds difficult (that must be tough).

大変です（ね）。

taihen desu (ne).
hard

That's a problem.

問題です（ね）。

mondai desu (ne).
problem

That looks interesting.

面白そうです（ね）。

omoshiro-sō desu (ne).
interesting looks

I can't (don't) believe it.

信じられないです。

shinjirarenai desu.
can't believe (to believe: shinjimasu)

There's no help for it (it can't be helped).

しょうがないです。

shō ga nai desu.
no help (nothing to be done)

Sorry for being late.

遅くなってすみません。

osoku natte sumimasen.
has become late sorry

Sorry to keep you waiting.

お待たせしてすみません。

o-matase shite sumimasen.
make you wait (humble form)

I have a request. (I have something to ask of you)

お願いがあるんです。

o-negai ga aru'n desu.
request

Do you have a minute (could I talk to you for a minute)?

ちょっとよろしいですか？

chotto yoroshii desu ka?
a minute may I?

Do you have time?

お時間ありますか？

o-jikan arimasu ka?
time do you have?

Actually …(As a matter of fact)

じつは…

jitsu wa …

You decide (I'll leave it to you).

お任せします。

o-makase shimasu.
leave to (humble form; to leave up to : makasemasu)

Please leave it to me (you can count on me).

任せてください。

makasete kudasai.
please leave it to me

waza-waza
arigatō gozaimashita

Thank you (for going to the trouble).

わざわざすみません。

waza-waza sumimasen.
go to the trouble

waza-waza sumimasen is a very handy phrase. You can use it in place of arigatō when someone gives you something or does something nice for you. waza-waza can also be attached to arigatō gozaimashita.

PRACTICE

Fill in the blanks below with the appropriate pocket phrase.

❶ Friend: Oh, I didn't know it was closed today.

あ、きょう休みだったのを知らなかった。

a, kyō yasumi datta no o shiranakatta.

(yasumi datta = was closed; shiranakatta = didn't know)

Pole-san: Too bad, huh!

_______ ね！

_______ ne!

❷ Friend: It's been a long time, hasn't it!

_______ ね！

_______ ne!

Pole-san: How have you been?

お元気でしたか？

o-genki deshita ka?

❸ Friend: Miss Yamada is getting married, huh.

山田さん結婚するんですね。

Yamada-san kekkon suru'n desu ne.

(kekkon suru'n desu = wil get married)

Pole-san: Yes, that's what they're saying (I heard that too).

_______ ね。

_______ ne.

❹ Friend: What do you think of the new proposal?

新しい提案 _______？

atarashii tēan _______?

❺ Pole-san: (arriving 15 minutes after the appointed time)
I'm sorry to be late!

_______!

_______!

❻ Friend: Tomorrow there is supposed to be a typhoon.

あした台風が来るみたいですね。

ashita taifū ga <u>kuru mitai</u> desu ne.

tomorrow will come, I hear

Pole-san: Oh, I hope there isn't!

_______!

_______!

❼ Friend: Next week there's a festival in the neighborhood.

来週近所でお祭りがあります。

raishū kinjo de o-matsuri ga arimasu.

next week festival there is/are

Pole-san: That sounds interesting!

_______ ね！

_______ ne!

❽ Friend: The president and vice-president don't get along at all.

社長と副社長は仲が悪いですね。

shachō to fuku-shachō wa <u>naka ga warui desu</u> ne.

president vice-president do not get along

Pole-san: That's a problem, huh.

_______ ね。

_______ ne.

❾ Pole-san: (greeting a client)

Thank you for coming today (thank you for going to the trouble of coming here)!

きょうは _______。

kyō wa _______.

---

answers ❶ zannen desu ❷ o-hisashiburi desu
❸ sō rashii desu ❹ dō omoimasu ka
❺ osoku natte sumimasen ❻ sō ja nai to ii desu
❼ omoshiro-sō desu ❽ mondai desu
❾ waza-waza sumimasen

"wide face, light mouth"?

The other day I overheard an interesting conversation between two young women on the train. One of them asked, "What's your new boss like?" Her friend replied, "Well, his face is wide, and his head is soft, but his mouth is a little light." Were they speaking in code?

There are a lot of interesting and commonly used expressions in Japanese that incorporate words for different parts of the body. There are actually more than 140 that use the word "eye" (目 **me**)! Knowing some of these can help spice up your conversation (and also give you a better idea of what people are talking about on the train!).

Hirayama

phrases related to the body

Idiomatic phrases combining adjectives (usually i-adjectives) with words for body parts are common in Japanese. The basic pattern is "body part + ga + adjective."

i-ADJECTIVES

good	bad	old	painful	hard
いい	悪い	古い	痛い	かたい
ii	warui	furui	itai	katai
soft	wide	fast	high	
柔らかい	広い	はやい	高い	
yawarakai	hiroi	hayai	takai	

1. phrases related to the head

head 頭 atama

bright; smart; sharp
頭がいい
atama ga ii

worried
頭が痛い
atama ga itai

not smart (thick-headed)
頭が悪い
atama ga warui

inflexible; stubborn
頭がかたい
atama ga katai

old-fashioned
頭が古い
atama ga furui

flexible (receptive to new things)
頭が柔らかい
atama ga yawarakai

II. phrases related to the face

face 顔 kao

have a wide circle of acquaintances

顔が広い

kao ga hiroi

III. phrases related to the ears

ears 耳 mimi

quick-eared; have sharp ears

耳がはやい

mimi ga hayai

ashamed to hear

耳が痛い

mimi ga itai

IV. phrases related to the nose

nose 鼻 hana

haughty (snobbish)

鼻が高い

hana ga takai

V. phrases related to the eyes

eyes 目 me

have an expert eye for

目がいい

me ga ii

VI. phrases related to the mouth

mouth 口 kuchi

can keep a secret; closed-mouthed

口がかたい

kuchi ga katai

have a sharp tongue; have a bad mouth

口が悪い

kuchi ga warui

PRACTICE

Fill in each blank below with a phrase from the list above.

❶ Kids' education is a real worry, isn't it?

子供の教育は ______ ですね。

kodomo no kyōiku wa ______ desu ne.
children education isn't it?

❷ You know all sorts of people. You seem to have a wide circle of acquaintances.

いろいろな人を知っていますね。______ ですね。

iroiro na hito o shitte imasu ne. ______ desu ne.
various people know

❸ What? You've already heard that rumor? My, you've got quick ears (nothing gets past you)!

えっ？もうそのうわさを知っていますか。______ ですね。

e? mō sono uwasa o shitte imasu ka. ______ desu ne.
huh? already rumor know

❹ Oh no, scolded again for the same thing! This is embarrassing.

あ、また言われました。______ です。

a, mata iwaremashita. ______ desu.
again was told

❺ That person can keep secrets, so please don't worry.

あの人は ______ ですから安心して下さい。

ano hito wa ______ desu kara anshin shite kudasai.
that person please stop worrying

❻ He is a good person, but he has a sharp tongue.

いい人なんです。でも ______ です。

ii hito nan desu. demo ______ desu.
good person but

---

answers ❶ atama ga itai ❷ kao ga hiroi ❸ mimi ga hayai
❹ mimi ga itai ❺ kuchi ga katai ❻ kuchi ga warui

KANJI PRACTICE

Kanji characters were first imported to Japan from China in about the third or fourth century A.D. Today Japanese uses about 5,000 characters and, of these, about 600 are ideographic, or meant to be depictions of the objects to which they refer. These are the kanji that Japanese learn first.

The following are a few of those ideographic kanji, most of them representing various parts of the body. Can you guess the meaning of each from the shape? In the boxes at right, copy the kanji from the selection given above that best resembles the image described by the English word at the left.

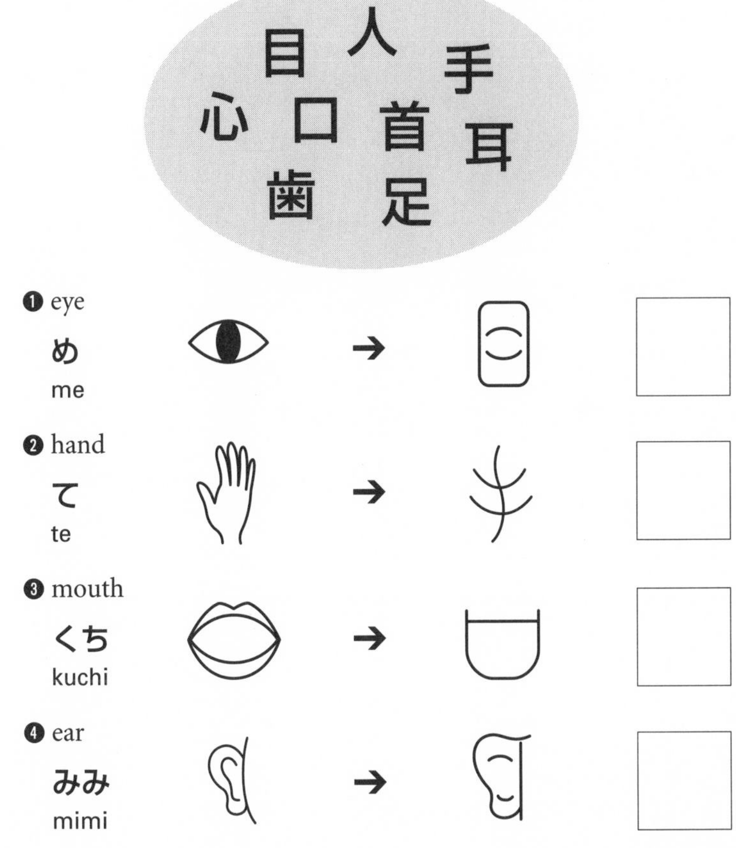

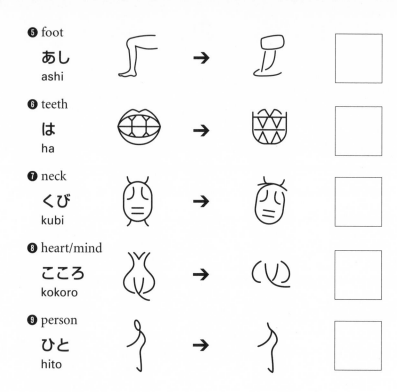

❺ foot

あし

ashi

❻ teeth

は

ha

❼ neck

くび

kubi

❽ heart/mind

こころ

kokoro

❾ person

ひと

hito

answers ❶目 ❷手 ❸口 ❹耳 ❺足 ❻歯 ❼首 ❽心 ❾人

wakarimasen or **shirimasen** "I don't know" the difference!

Mr. Pole

When I want to say, "I don't know" in Japanese, I always use **shirimasen**. But I've noticed that a lot of Japanese people say **wakarimasen** much more often. These two phrases are supposed to have the same meaning, so what exactly is the difference? Is **wakarimasen** more polite? I'm afraid that I may have been using **shirimasen** in inappropriate situations.

As you say, the two words have basically the same meaning. But there is a difference: if you use **shirimasen** in conversation, it can sound cold or unfeeling in some cases. The information on the next page will help to clarify the two phrases. But when it's not clear to you which one to use, it may be safer to say **wakarimasen**.

Hirayama

two verbs for "I don't know": shirimasen, wakarimasen

知りません

shirimasen can be used to give an objective answer to a factual, yes-or-no question. It means, "I don't have any knowledge/information."

Q: Do you know Mr. Kijima?
木島さんを知っていますか？
Kijima-san o shitte imasu ka?

A: No, I don't know him.
いいえ、知りません。
iie, shirimasen.

(In this case, shirimasen implies "I simply don't know him at all"/"I haven't met him"/"I don't have any information about him," etc.)

Be careful not to use shirimasen too often or in a forceful tone, or you will sound indifferent and unconcerned.

わかりません

wakarimasen can be used in nearly any situation. It means, "I don't know," "I have no idea," "I can't figure it out," etc. Unlike shirimasen, there is no danger of your sounding cold when you use this word.

Q: $\sqrt{5} \div 0.215 \times 8 \div 24 = ?$

A: I don't know.
わかりません。
wakarimasen. (implies "I have no idea")

Q: When is this company on summer holiday?
会社の夏休みはいつですか？
kaisha no natsuyasumi wa itsu desu ka?

A: I don't know.

わかりません。

wakarimasen. (implies "I should know, but I don't")

Use wakarimasen for knowledge that comes through the five senses: sight, hearing, smell, taste, or touch.

SIGHT Q: How high is that mountain?

あの山の高さは？

ano yama no takasa wa?
that mountain height

HEARING Q: Is this the sound of a harpsichord or a piano?

これはハープシコードの音？ ピアノの音？

kore wa *harpsichord* no oto? *piano* no oto?
this sound

SMELL Q: Something smells good. Is that yakitori?

いいにおいですね。焼き鳥？

ii nioi desu ne. yakitori?
smell grilled chicken

TASTE Q: Is this wine cabernet?

このワインはカベルネですか？

kono *wine* wa *cabernet* desu ka?

TOUCH Q: Is this carpet (made of) wool?

このカーペットはウールですか？

kono *carpet* wa *wool* desu ka?

wakarimasen can be used to answer all of the above questions.

thssssss … wakarimasen

When they want to show that they are thinking about something, Japanese people sometimes make a thsssss sound, by abruptly sucking in their breath through their teeth in what might be called a long, backward hiss.

PRACTICE

Fill in the blanks below with either shirimasen or wakarimasen.

Client: I hear you're going to Kyoto next week.

来週京都に行くそうですね。

raishū Kyoto ni iku-sō desu ne.
next week go I heard

Are you staying in a hotel or an inn?

ホテルですか、それとも旅館ですか？

hotel desu ka, soretomo ryokan desu ka?
or inn

Mr. Pole: Hmm … I don't know. 2 forms

___❶___. (implying "I am still thinking about it")

___❷___. (implying "someone else is making the decision")

Client: Do you know a good fish restaurant in Kyoto?

京都で魚のおいしいレストランご存知ですか。

Kyoto de sakana no oishii *restaurant* go-zonji desu ka?
do you know? (polite form)

Mr. Pole: Hmm … I don't know. 2 forms

___❸___. (implying "I don't know anything about restaurants in Kyoto")

___❹___. (implying "I know a good restaurant in Kyoto but it is not a fish restaurant")

---

answers ❶ wakarimasen ❷ shirimasen ❸ shirimasen ❹ wakarimasen

the kanji for **shirimasu**

知

chi: knowing, awareness, intelligence
shi(ru): to know

as far as I know

私の知っている限りでは
watashi no shitte iru kagiri dewa

naïve, ignorant of the ways of the world

世間知らず
sekenshirazu

acquaintances

知り合い
shiriai

degree of fame

知名度
chimēdo

PRACTICE

Fill in the blanks below with the correct expression from above.

❶ This product is not well known but somehow it manages to sell well.

この商品は ______ が低いですが、なぜかよく売れています。

kono shōhin wa ______ ga hikui desu ga, nazeka yoku urete imasu.
product / low / for some reason / selling

❷ My father has a wide circle of acquaintances, so heaps of New Year's cards come for him.

父は ______ が多いので年賀状が山のように来ます。

chichi wa ______ ga ōi node nengajō ga yama no yōni kimasu.
my father / many so / New Year's cards like mountains / come

❸ As far as I know, it has nothing to do with that person.

______ あの人は関係ないですよ。

______ ano hito wa kankē nai desu yo.
that person / no connection

❹ My son has gotten a job, but he still knows nothing about the world.

息子は社会人になったけどまだまだ ______ です。

musuko wa shakaijin ni natta kedo mada mada ______ desu.
my son working person became but still

answers ❶ chimēdo ❷ shiriai ❸ watashi no shiru kagiri dewa ❹ sekenshirazu

TALK

The following dialog illustrates natural usages of shirimasen and wakarimasen while also introducing new expressions.

Nakata-san: I ran into Yamada-san at the supermarket and I said hi to her, but she **acted like she hadn't seen me at all**! I wonder why.

スーパーで山田さんを見かけたので声をかけたら**知らんぷり**されちゃった。どうしてかな？

super(market) de Yamada-san o mikaketa node koe o kaketara **shiran-puri** sarechatta. dō shite ka na?
when I spoke to why I wonder

(sarechatta here is an abbreviated, colloquial version of sarete-shimaimashita—a passive form used to indicate that one has been ill affected by somebody/something.)

Kitazawa-san: Huh? But **didn't you know** that Yamada-san had plastic surgery?

え？ 山田さん整形したのを**知らなかったの**？

e? Yamada-san sēkē shita no o **shiranakatta** no?
had plastic surgery

(no often replaces ka as a marker of questions, in which case it is pronounced with rising intonation)

Nakata-san: What! No, **I had no idea**!

え? **全然知らなかった**!

e? **zenzen shiranakatta**!

not at all

So maybe that's why **she pretended like she didn't see me;** she was embarrassed.

恥ずかしかったので、**知らんぷり**したのかな。

hazukashikatta node, **shiran-puri** shita no ka na.

was embarrassed because I wonder

Kitazawa-san: **Did you know** she had her breasts done too?

胸の整形は**知っている**?

mune no sēkē wa **shitte iru**?

chest/bust

Nakata-san: Oh **yeah, yeah, I knew** about that.

うん**知ってる知ってる**。

un **shitteru shitteru**.

(The i before the ru in shitte iru is often dropped in colloquial Japanese.)

Kitazawa-san: I wonder what she'll have done next!

次はどこを整形するのかなあ?

tsugi wa doko o sēkē suru no ka nā?

next where I wonder

Nakata-san: Sometimes **I don't understand her at all**!

あの人のする事はいつも**訳がわからない**。

ano hito no suru koto wa itsumo **wake ga wakaranai**.

the things she does

(wake ga wakaranai is a casual, colloquial expression. It has the nuance of "is (totally) illogical." wakaranai.)

Kitazawa-san: Me neither!

ほんと!

honto!

(an abbreviated version of hontō, meaning "Truly!" "Indeed!" or "You can say that again!")

"ate a restaurant"?

Mr. Pole

During a lunch break with some colleagues, I was reading through a gourmet magazine and saw a listing for my favorite restaurant. I told my friends, **kinō kono oishii *restaurant* o tabemashita**. I meant to say, "I ate yesterday at this delicious restaurant," but they all started laughing. One of them asked, "How was it? Was it good?"

They were laughing because you used the wrong particle when you spoke. What you actually said was "I ate this restaurant" (***restaurant* o tabemashita**). You should have used the particle **de** instead of **o**, saying, ***restaurant* de tabemashita**. Maybe what you need is some help with sentence structure and deciding which particle to use. First let's look at the particle **wa**, which is perhaps the most basic.

Hirayama

は

There are a lot of different ways to use the particle wa, but two of the most common are 1) to give details about something and 2) to imply a comparison with other things.

1) Using wa to give details or explain:

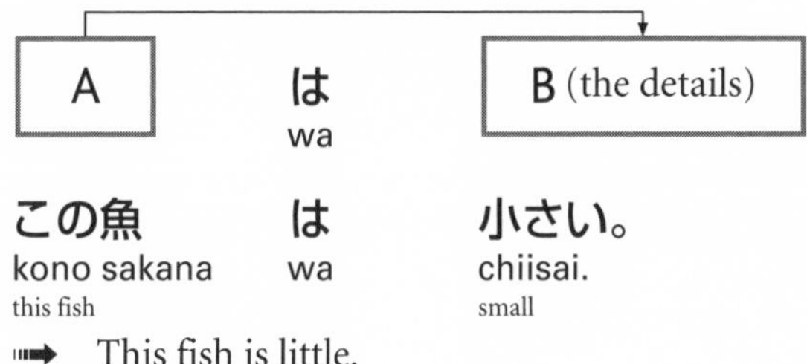

"A will now be explained by B"

B (the details)

kono sakana
this fish

➡ This fish is little.

2) Using wa to imply a comparison with other things (to make a relative statement):

"A will now be compared with something else"

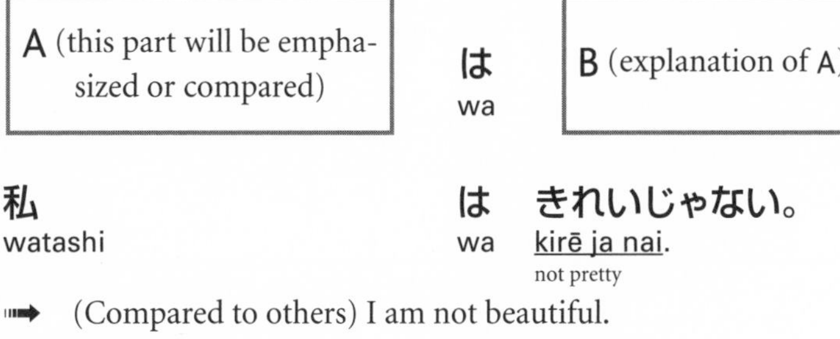

B (explanation of A)

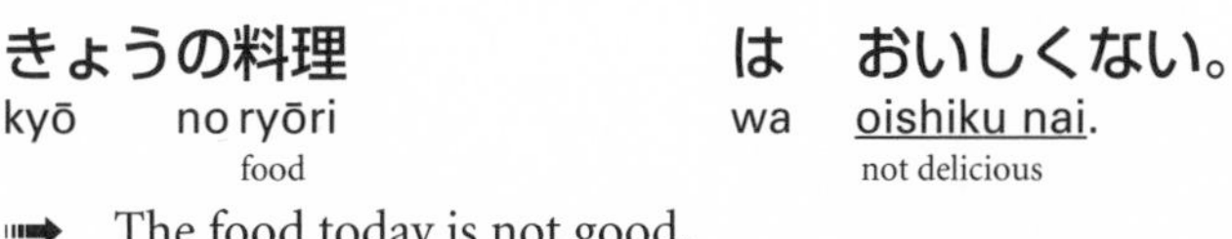

A (this part will be emphasized or compared)

きれいじゃない。
kirē ja nai.
not pretty
➡ (Compared to others) I am not beautiful.

きょうの料理
kyō no ryōri
food
は
wa
おいしくない。
oishiku nai.
not delicious
➡ The food today is not good.

When you use wa, your listeners will expect and anticipate details.

あの人 は [ ] People expect details at this point!
ano hito wa
that person

wa with dates

wa is not usually used after words that are related to dates, like ashita (tomorrow), asatte (the day after tomorrow), nichiyōbi (Sunday), raishū (next week), etc.

I'm going to see my friend tomorrow.

あした ~~は~~ 友達に会います。
ashita ~~wa~~ tomodachi ni aimasu.
tomorrow friend meet

In some cases, you could have a wa here, but more often you would not. If you do not have wa, it's a simple sentence meaning "I will see my friend tomorrow." But if you add wa right after ashita, this places the emphasis of the sentence on "tomorrow"—tomorrow as opposed to any other time. So with wa, this sentence could mean "It's tomorrow that I'm going to see a friend." Or "I have a plan tomorrow; it's to go see my friend" (implied is, "Tomorrow I have this plan, but as for other days …")

あした は 友達に会います。
ashita wa tomodachi ni aimasu.

o

o marks the direct object of a sentence.

I ate expensive tempura.

高い天ぷらを食べました。

takai tempura o tabemashita.

expensive ate

de

de indicates the place at which an action occurs.

Yesterday I had dinner at a good restaurant.

きのう、おいしいレストランで食べました。

kinō, oishii *restaurant* de tabemashita.

yesterday at ate

ni

ni indicates location, time, or the direction of an action.

It's in the coin locker.

コインロッカーにあります。

coin locker ni arimasu.

exist, be

The movie starts at 5 o'clock.

映画は5時に始まります。

ēga wa go-ji ni hajimarimasu.

movie 5 o'clock start

Let's get on/ride the bus.

バスに乗りましょう。

bus ni norimashō.
let's get on

Like **de**, **ni** can also mark the location of an action. However, actions associated with **ni** are usually continuous: living, being employed, etc.

I live in Tokyo.

東京に住んでいます。

Tokyo ni sunde imasu.
am living

I work at a securities company.

証券会社に勤めています。

shōken-gaisha ni tsutomete imasu.
securities company work, be employed

PARTICLE QUIZ

Make three complete sentences for each set of words below by drawing a line from each particle in the middle column to the phrase on the right that fits with it. The first set has been done for you.

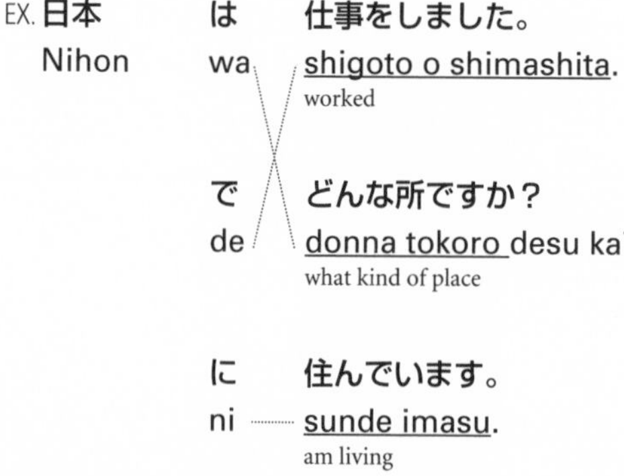

❶ 天ぷら tempura	と to	作りました。 tsukurimashita. made
	を o	寿司が好きです。 sushi ga suki desu. like
	は wa	2500円です。 nisen gohyaku-en desu.

❷ 車 kuruma car	で de	来ました。 kimashita. came
	を o	乗りませんでした。 norimasen deshita. didn't ride
	に ni	売りました。 urimashita. sold

❸ 友達 tomodachi friend	を o	誕生日プレゼントをあげましたか？ tanjōbi *present* o agemashita ka? birthday / did you give?
	に ni	食事をしました。 shokuji o shimashita. had a meal
	と to	招待しました。 shōtai shimashita. invited

❹ 新宿 に 映画を見ましたか？
Shinjuku ni ēga o mimashita ka?
movie watched

は 行きました。
wa ikimashita.
went

で 人が多いです。
de hito ga ōi desu.
people a lot of

---

answers

EX. Nihon	wa	donna tokoro desu ka? (What sort of place is Japan?)
	de	shigoto o shimashita. (I worked in Japan.)
	ni	sunde imasu. (I am living in Japan.)
❶ tempura	to	sushi ga suki desu. (I like tempura and sushi.)
	o	tsukurimashita. (I made tempura.)
	wa	nisen gohyaku-en desu. (Tempura is 2500 yen.)
❷ kuruma	de	kimashita. (I came by car.)
	o	urimashita. (I sold my car.)
	ni	norimasen deshita. (I didn't get in the car.)
❸ tomodachi	o	shōtai shimashita. (I invited my friend.)
	ni	tanjōbi *present* o agemashita ka? (Did you give your friend a birthday present?)
	to	shokuji o shimashita. (I had a meal with my friend.)
❹ Shinjuku	ni	ikimashita. (I went to Shinjuku.)
	wa	hito ga ōi desu. (In Shinjuku there are a lot of people.)
	de	ēga o mimashita ka? (In Shinjuku did you see a movie?)

a basic rule of sentence structure: word order is up to you!

Japanese grammar places less emphasis on word order than other languages do. Although it's up to you to decide how to arrange your words, it will be much easier to communicate in Japanese if you start each sentence with the most important idea ("the large"), then work down through the less important elements ("the small") and finish with the verb. The only restrictions to this rule of thumb are that the particles must stay with the words they modifiy and the verb must come last.

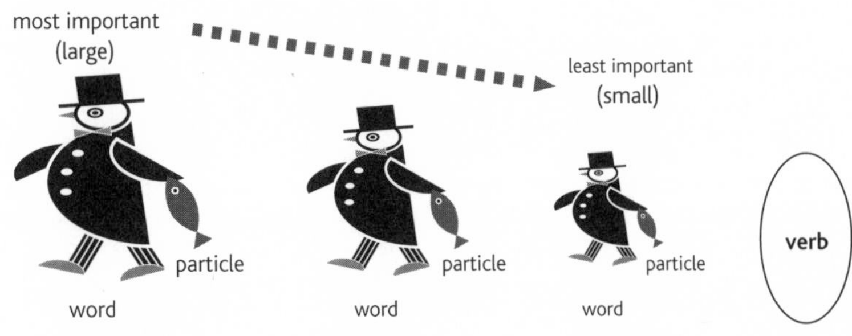

You decide on the word order!

Below are three different ways to say, "I'm going to see my friend in Hawaii next week." All are correct, and they are just different in what part of the sentence they emphasize. (NOTE: In general, Japanese people do not use "I (**watashi**)" much in everyday speech. Using **watashi** too often can sound arrogant. Avoid using it except in cases when you want to emphasize yourself.)

~~私は~~ ~~watashi wa~~	ハワイで *Hawaii* de	来週 raishū next week	友達に tomodachi ni friend	会います。 aimasu. will meet
	来週 raishū	ハワイで *Hawaii* de	友達に tomodachi ni	会います。 aimasu.
	友達に tomodachi ni	来週 raishū	ハワイで *Hawaii* de	会います。 aimasu.

large-to-small rule

Basically, in Japanese sentences, the "large" idea is expressed first, with smaller ideas following. This "large-to-small rule" also applies to many other situations in Japanese, e.g.:

1) Family name first, given name last;

I'm Tomomi Tanaka.

田中友美です。

Tanaka Tomomi desu.
(family name) (given name)

2) Company name first, then department, then your name;

My name is John Gold. I work in the personnel department at Japanese Lunch.

ジャパニーズランチ人事部のジョン・ゴールドです。

Japanese Lunch jinjibu no *John Gold* desu.

3) Postal addresses are given in this order: prefecture, city, ward, street address, building name, apartment number, and, finally, your name. So, for the address of John Gold, at Japanese Lunch, the order would be:

東京都渋谷区南 2-3-3 サンシャインビル206
ジャパニーズランチ株式会社

ジョン・ゴールド様

Tokyo-to Shibuya-ku Minami 2–3–3 Sunshine Bldg. #206
Japanese Lunch Co., Ltd.

John Gold-sama

4) Dates and times are also given from largest unit to smallest. So 5:05:05 on Thursday, September 10, 2010 would be:

2010年 9月10日 木曜日 5時5分5秒

nisen jū-nen ku-gatsu tōka mokuyōbi go-ji go-fun go-byō
2010 September 10 Thursday 5 o'clock, 5 minutes, 5 seconds

watashi ga! watashi ga! watashi ga!

Mr. Pole

I saw an interesting thing in a restaurant the other day. Two Japanese businessmen were each trying to grab the bill from the other, saying, **watashi ga**! **watashi ga**! I'm familiar with **watashi,** but I hadn't really thought much about the meaning of **ga** before. But I figured **watashi ga** was something people say when leaving a restaurant. So I went out to eat with a Japanese friend a few days later, and when the bill came, I grabbed it and said **watashi ga**! But he just said **gochisōsama**, Pole-**san** ("Thanks for the meal!") and walked away! I hadn't said anything about paying!

The problem is your particles again. Here **ga** is used to emphasize a particular thing—in this case, **watashi**, meaning "It is **I** [who will pay the bill]." Even though you didn't say anything overtly about paying, your choice of words clearly suggested to your friend that you wanted to pay!

Hirayama

が

There are many ways to use **ga**, as the following examples indicate.

1) To select something out of a group:

I like tuna. (selecting something that one likes)

マグロが好きです。

maguro ga suki desu.
tuna like

(implies "out of the entire category of fish, it is tuna that I like.")

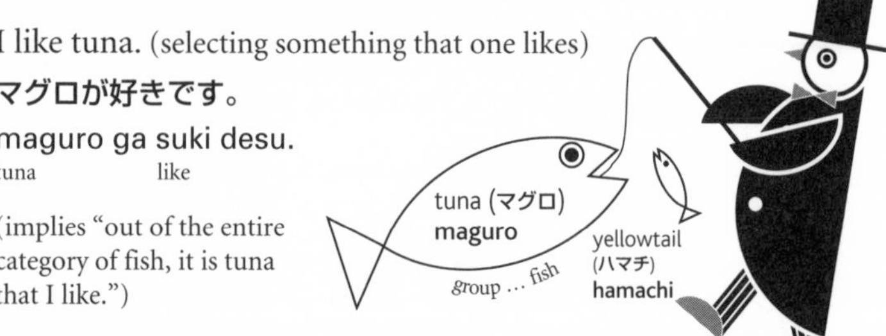

There's Mrs. Mori. (selecting someone ➡ "there is/are …")

森さんがいます。

Mori-san ga imasu.
exist

Sunday is good for me. (selecting from among possibilities)

日曜日がいいです。

nichiyōbi ga ii desu.
Sunday good

I want a day off. (selecting from among desires)

休みが欲しいです。

yasumi ga hoshii desu.
day off want

2) To emphasize an occurrence:

There was an accident.

事故がありました。

jiko ga arimashita.
accident there was

3) To emphasize an ability:

I can ski.

スキーができます。

ski ga dekimasu.
can

4) In responding to "where" (doko), "when" (itsu), "what" (nani), and "who" (dare) questions, ga marks the answer:

Q: When would you like to go on the trip?

旅行はいつがいいですか？

ryokō wa itsu ga ii desu ka?
trip when good

A: I'd like to go next month.

来月がいいですね。

raigetsu ga ii desu ne.
next month good

Q: What's a good restaurant (which restaurant is good)?

どこの店がおいしいですか？

doko no mise ga oishii desu ka?
where restaurant delicious

A: The one in front of the train station is good.

駅前の店がおいしいですよ。

eki-mae no mise ga oishii desu yo.
in front of station I tell you

Q: What is important in (your) life?

人生で何が大切ですか？

jinsē de nani ga taisetsu desu ka?
human life what important

A: (Good) health is important.

健康が大切です。

kenkō ga taisetsu desu.
health

Q: Who is coming to the meeting?

会議に誰が来ますか？

kaigi ni dare ga kimasu ka?
meeting who will come

A: Mr. Koga is coming.

古賀さんが来ます。

Koga-san ga kimasu.

5) ga is also used with intransitive verbs that describe an action or occurrence, such as the verbs for, for instance, "to come out" (demasu), "to break down" (kowaremasu), "to increase" (fuemasu), "to blow" (fukimasu), "to spill (out)" (koboremasu), or "to cry" (nakimasu):

The wind is blowing.

風が吹いています。

kaze ga fuite imasu.
wind

The cat is meowing.

猫が鳴いています。

neko ga naite imasu.
cat meowing

NOTE: You may also sometimes hear a different ga used in conversation. In addition to the particle ga, there is also a different ga that is a transitional expression used to link two sentences. This ga means "but."

It's raining out, but it will probably stop soon.

雨が降っていますが、すぐやむでしょう。

ame ga futte imasu ga, sugu yamu deshō.
rain is falling but soon probably stop

PRACTICE

Fill in the blanks with either **wa** or **ga**, as appropriate. Remember that **ga** is used for selecting or emphasizing, and **wa** for giving details. (See pp. 85–86 for more on **wa**.)

Colleague: Who is going to Paris in Mr. Mori's place?

誰 ______ 森さんのかわりにパリに行きますか？

dare __❶__ Mori-san <u>no kawari ni</u> *Paris* ni ikimasu ka?
who / instead of / will go

Pole-san: Mr. Koga is going.

古賀さん ______ 行きます。

Koga-san __❷__ ikimasu.

Colleague: What kind of person is Mr. Koga?

古賀さん ______ どんな人ですか？

Koga-san __❸__ donna hito desu ka?
what kind of

Pole-san: Mr. Koga is an accountant and he is very smart.

古賀さん ______ 会計士で 頭 ______ いいです。

Koga-san __❹__ kaikēshi de atama __❺__ ii desu.
accountant / head / good (sharp)

Colleague: But Mr. Mori was actually supposed to go, right?

本当は森さん ______ 行くはずでしたね。

hontō wa Mori-san __❻__ <u>iku hazu</u> deshita ne.
the truth is / supposed to go

Pole-san: Yes, but the work Mr. Mori is doing now is late so he can't go.

ええ、でも森さん ______ 今の仕事 ______ 遅れていますので 行けません。

ē, demo Mori-san __❼__ ima no shigoto __❽__
but / present / work

<u>okurete imasu</u> node ikemasen.
being late / cannot go

(continuing)

But if Mr. Koga goes, everything should be fine.

古賀さん ______ 行けば全てうまくいくでしょう。

Koga-san ___❾___ ikeba subete umaku iku deshō.

if he goes everything will probably go well

Colleague: I'm glad to hear that.

それを聞いて安心しました。

sore o kiite anshin shimashita.

that hear feel at ease (stop worrying)

answers
❶ ga (answers "who")
❷ ga (selecting a person out of a group)
❸ wa (asking for details about)
❹ wa (giving details about)
❺ ga (selecting characteristics about Mr. Koga)
❻ ga (selecting Mr. Mori from among the staff)
❼ wa (giving details about Mr. Mori)
❽ ga (selecting the cause of Mr. Mori's situation)
❾ ga (selecting Mr. Koga from among the staff)

PARTICLE QUIZ

Make complete sentences for each set of words below by drawing a line from each particle in the middle column to the phrase on the right that fits with it. The first set has been done for you.

EX. 会社 kaisha company	に ni	車で行きます。 kuruma de ikimasu. car will go
	を o	倒産しました。 tōsan shimashita. went bankrupt
	が ga	来月辞めたいです。 raigetsu yametai desu. next month want to quit

❶ これ
kore
(this)

は　これお願いします。
wa　kore o-negai shimasu.
　　this please

と　何ですか？
to　nan desu ka?
　　what

が　好きです。
ga　suki desu.
　　like

を　900円で買いました。
o　kyūhyaku-en de kaimashita.
　　900 yen for bought

❷ 電話
denwa
telephone

を　します。
o　shimasu.
　　do

が　誰も出ません。
ga　daremo demasen.
　　no one answers

に　鳴っています。
ni　natte imasu.
　　is ringing

と　メールとどちらが便利ですか？
to　*mail* to dochira ga benri desu ka?
　　which convenient

❸ トイレ
toilet

に　誰か入っています。
ni　dareka haitte imasu.
　　someone is in

が　こわれています。
ga　kowarete imasu.
　　is broken

を　ちょっとお借りしたいんですが。
o　chotto o-kari shitai'n desu ga.
　　a moment want to use (humble form)

❹ 蜂 hachi (bee)

に ni — とりました。 torimashita. (caught)

を o — 刺されました。 sasaremashita. (was bitten)

が ga — います。 imasu. (there is)

❺ 窓 mado (window)

を o — 開けて下さい。 akete kudasai. (please open)

から kara — 開きませんでした。 akimasen deshita. (didn't open)

が ga — 富士山が見えます。 Fuji-san ga miemasu. (Mt. Fuji — can be seen)

---

answers

EX. kaisha
- ni — kuruma de ikimasu. (I go to work by car.)
- o — raigetsu yametai desu. (I would like to quit the company next month.)
- ga — tōsan shimashita. (The company went bankrupt.)

❶ kore
- wa — nan desu ka? (What is this?)
- to — kore o-negai shimasu. (I would like this and this please.)
- ga — suki desu. (I like this.)
- o — kyūhyaku-en de kaimashita. (I bought this for 900 yen.)

❷ denwa
- o — shimasu. (I will make a telephone call.)
- ga — natte imasu. (The telephone is ringing.)
- ni — daremo demasen. (No one answers [the phone].)
- to — *mail* to dochira ga benri desu ka? (Which is more convenient, telephone or e-mail?)

❸ *toilet*	ni	dareka haitte imasu. (Someone is in the bathroom.)
	ga	kowarete imasu. (The toilet is broken.)
	o	chotto o-kari shitai'n desu ga. (I would like to use the bathroom for a moment.)
❹ hachi	ni	sasaremashita. (I was bitten by a bee.)
	o	torimashita. (I caught a bee.)
	ga	imasu. (There is a bee.)
❺ mado	o	akete kudasai. (Please open the window.)
	kara	Fuji-san ga miemasu. (I can see Mt. Fuji from the window.)
	ga	akimasen deshita. (The window didn't open.)

omitting particles

At times when you don't understand which particle to use, you can generally leave the particle out. Japanese often do this as a way of shortening their speech. So for instance:

I like animals.

動物が好きです。 ➡ 動物好きです。

dōbutsu ga suki desu. ➡ dōbutsu-zuki desu.

animals like

Yesterday I bought a book.

きのう本を買いました。 ➡ きのう本買いました。

kinō hon o kaimashita. ➡ kinō hon kaimashita.

book bought

The only particle that you shouldn't omit is de, since doing so will usually cause confusion.

I will go by car. ➡ Car will go.

車で行きます。 ➡ ~~車行きます。~~

kuruma de ikimasu. ➡ ~~kuruma ikimasu.~~

car will go

What day is **donichi**?

Mr. Pole

My friends and I were making plans to go to an onsen (a hot spring) together. One of them asked me, **donichi isogashii desu ka**? ("Are you busy on **donichi**?") I didn't know what **donichi** meant, but I didn't want to admit that, so I told her I would be busy. Another friend had told us that **donichi** was better for her, but my friend made reservations for us to go on a weekday. I wanted to go on a weekend, too. Why did she choose a weekday? What is **donichi**?

I think students of Japanese probably say **getsuyōbi to suiyōbi** when they mean to say "Monday and Wednesday." But Japanese people would use a shorter term for this, **ges-sui**, which is a combination of the first syllables of **getsuyōbi** and **suiyōbi**. So as you have no doubt figured out by now, **donichi** is the combination of **doyōbi** (Saturday) and **nichiyōbi** (Sunday). Your friend must have thought you were busy on weekends. In the future maybe you should try asking about the words you don't understand. A good way to ask is just to repeat the word (**donichi**?) with a quizzical look on your face.

Hirayama

kanji for the days of the week

As we have seen, some kanji characters are ideographic (see p. 77). In Japanese, the days of the week are all ideographic. Or actually, the first kanji of each day of the week is ideographic. Each day of the week ends in yōbi 曜日 (equivalent to the English "day"). It's a good idea to at least familiarize yourself with the shapes of the characters for the days of the week, since they are often used in everyday life and in business.

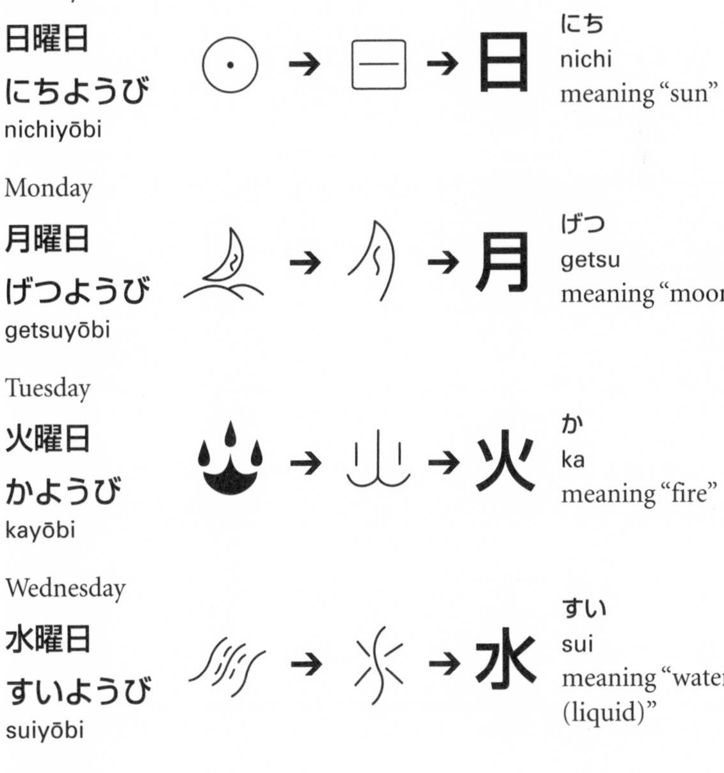

Sunday

日曜日
にちようび
nichiyōbi

→ → 日

にち
nichi
meaning "sun"

Monday

月曜日
げつようび
getsuyōbi

→ → 月

げつ
getsu
meaning "moon"

Tuesday

火曜日
かようび
kayōbi

→ → 火

か
ka
meaning "fire"

Wednesday

水曜日
すいようび
suiyōbi

→ → 水

すい
sui
meaning "water (liquid)"

Thursday

木曜日
もくようび
mokuyōbi

→ → 木

もく
moku
meaning "trees (plants/wood)"

Friday

金曜日

きんようび

kinyōbi

→ → 金

きん

kin

meaning "gold (money/metal)"

Saturday

土曜日

どようび

doyōbi

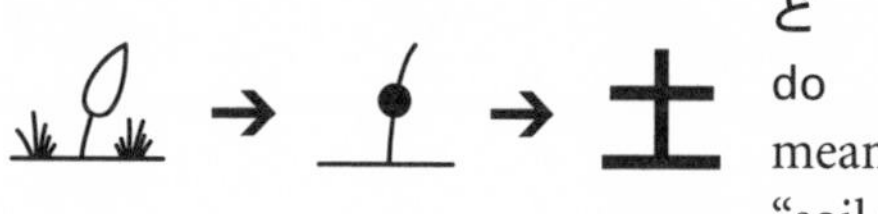

ど

do

meaning "soil (land)"

PRACTICE

Try sounding out the shortened forms for the following day-of-the-week combinations. The pronunciations for the days of the week are: **getsu/ge** (Monday), **kā/ka** (Tuesday), **sui** (Wednesday), **moku** (Thursday), **kin** (Friday), **dō/do** (Saturday), and **nichi** (Sunday).

❶ Friday & Saturday ______

❷ Tuesday & Friday ______

❸ Monday & Wednesday ______

❹ Monday & Thursday ______

answers ❶ kin-dō ❷ kā-kin/ka-kin ❸ ges-sui ❹ getsu-moku

phrases containing the kanji for the days of the week

everyday occurrences/daily happenings

日常茶飯事

nichijō-sahanji
daily tea meal

date of birth

生年月日

sēnen-gappi
birth year month day

Where there's smoke there's fire.

火のない所に煙は立たぬ

hi no nai tokoro ni kemuri wa tatanu
place without fire smoke doesn't rise

like oil and water/incompatible

水と油

mizu to abura
water and oil

can't see the forest for the trees

木を見て森を見ず

ki o mite mori o mizu
seeing trees not seeing forest (classical form)

Money comes and goes/Easy come, easy go

金は天下の回りもの

kane wa tenka no mawarimono
money the world round things

at the last minute/at the critical moment

土壇場

dotamba
soil platform place

PRACTICE

Fill in the blanks with phrases from the preceding page.

❶ Please write down the **date of your birth** here.

ここに ______ を書いて下さい。

koko ni ______ o kaite kudasai.
here please write

❷ I changed my mind **at the last minute**.

______ で気が変わりました。

______ de ki ga kawarimashita.
mind changed

❸ It is dangerous if you **can't see the forest for the trees**.

______ は危険です。

______ wa kiken desu.
dangerous

❹ Their quarrelling **is an everyday occurrence**.

あの人達の口げんかは ______ です。

ano hito-tachi no kuchi-genka wa ______ desu.
those people quarrel

❺ My husband and I get along well, even though our personalities are **like oil and water**.

私達夫婦は ______ ですけど、仲が良いです。

watashi-tachi fūfu wa ______ desu kedo, naka ga ii desu.
we husband and wife but get along well

❻ Don't be depressed! **Money comes and goes**, you know!

そんなに大きなため息をつかないで。 ______ ですよ！

sonnani ōki na tameiki o tsukanaide. ______ desu yo!
like that big sigh don't sigh

❼ I believe it is true, because **there's no smoke without fire**.

______ と言いますから本当でしょう。

______ to iimasu kara hontō deshō.
say true likely

answers ❶ sēnen-gappi ❷ dotamba ❸ ki o mite mori o mizu ❹ nichijō-sahanji ❺ mizu to abura ❻ kane wa tenka no mawarimono ❼ hi no nai tokoro ni kemuri wa tatanu

KANJI QUIZ

Here are some more ideographic kanji. Can you guess, from their shape, which is used to write each word in the list below? In the boxes at right, copy the kanji that best resembles the word described.

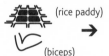

❶ man
おとこ
otoko

(rice paddy)
(biceps)
→

❷ child
こ(ども)
ko(domo)

→

❸ fish
さかな
sakana

→

❹ car
くるま
kuruma

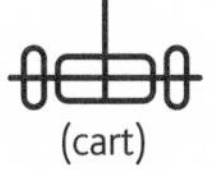
(cart)
→

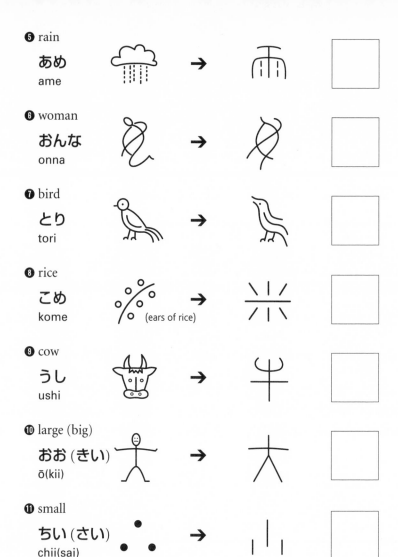

❺ rain

あめ

ame

❻ woman

おんな

onna

❼ bird

とり

tori

❽ rice

こめ

kome

(ears of rice)

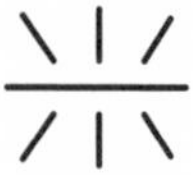

❾ cow

うし

ushi

❿ large (big)

おお (きい)

ō(kii)

⓫ small

ちい (さい)

chii(sai)

answers ❶男 ❷子 ❸魚 ❹車 ❺雨 ❻女 ❼鳥 ❽米 ❾牛 ❿大 ⓫小

-mashita is not always a past tense!

Mr. Pole

I've noticed that Japanese people often use past-tense verbs in confusing ways. For instance, they say **wakarimashita**, which sounds like it should mean "I understood," but actually seems to mean "I understand." One time I went mountain climbing with a friend and when we got to the top she said, **tsukaremashita** (which I guess means "I was tired"?). When was she tired? Why are people always talking in the past tense in Japanese?

Hirayama

I think that like most students of Japanese, you have studied the form **-mashita** and learned that it is the past tense of **-masu**. But what you also need to know is that **-mashita** is not always a past tense. It is also frequently used with certain verbs to describe an ongoing, present condition.

the past tense (-mashita) can describe present conditions

～ました

The past-tense (-mashita, or the more casual -ta form) can be used to describe a physical or mental condition, especially one that is occurring or that appears to be occurring at just the moment the -mashita phrase is spoken, e.g., "I feel … (at that moment)."

I'm so tired.

疲れました。 polite style OR 疲れた。 casual style

tsukaremashita. tsukareta.

(past tense of tsukaremasu: to become tired)

Here are some more examples. With any of these, the more casual -ta form can be substituted for -mashita.

I'm surprised.
おどろきました。
odorokimashita.

It bothers me. (I'm upset.)
困りました。
komarimashita.

I forgot.
忘れました。
wasuremashita.

I'm lost.
迷いました。
mayoimashita.

I understand.
わかりました。
wakarimashita.

I've gained weight.
太りました。
futorimashita.

I remember.
思い出しました。
omoidashimashita.

I've lost weight.
やせました。
yasemashita.

I've caught a cold.

風邪をひきました。

kaze o hikimashita.
cold

I'm thirsty.

のどが渇きました。

nodo ga kawakimashita.
throat got thirsty

I'm hungry.

おなかがすきました。

onaka ga sukimashita.
stomach got empty

The past-tense -mashita or -ta forms can also be used to describe things happening now: some activity, event, communication, or action.

The train is coming! (Here comes the train!)

あ、電車が来ました！

a, densha ga kimashita!
train

OR

あ、電車が来た！ casual style

a, densha ga kita!

use of the present participle to describe ongoing conditions

The present participle (-te form plus imasu or the more casual -te form plus iru) is used to describe conditions that are basically static or exist over a period of time.

I'm tired.

疲れています。

tsukarete imasu.

I remember.

覚えています。

oboete imasu.

I know. (I understand.)

わかっています。

wakatte imasu.

I know.

知っています。

shitte imasu.

I'm lost.

迷っています。

mayotte imasu.

I've gained weight. (I'm fat.)

太っています。

futotte imasu.

I've lost weight. (I'm thin.)

やせています。

yasete imasu.

I have a cold.

風邪をひいています。

kaze o hiite imasu.

I'm hungry.

おなかが空いています。

onaka ga suite imasu.

I'm thirsty.

のどが渇いています。

nodo ga kawaite imasu.

-mashita vs. **-te imasu**

To compare:

I'm tired (after some exertion)

疲れました。

tsukaremashita.

I'm tired (and I have been for hours/days/weeks/months, etc.)

疲れています。

tsukarete imasu.

I've caught a cold.

風邪をひきました。

kaze o hikimashita.

I have a cold.

風邪をひいています。

kaze o hiite imasu.

If you want to be clear about the fact that you did something or that something happened in the past, say when (last week, last month, etc.)

I caught a cold last month.

先月風邪をひきました。

sengetsu kaze o hikimashita.
last month

PRACTICE

Fill in the blanks with a verb in the -mashita or -te form plus imasu.

❶ Oh, it's already noon! I'm hungry!

うわあ、もう12時！＿＿＿＿。

uwā, mō jūni-ji! ＿＿＿＿.

oh boy already 12 o'clock

❷ Oh, I see! I understand!

ああ、そうだったのか。＿＿＿＿。 casual style

ā, sō datta no ka. ＿＿＿＿.

❸ You have a fever and are coughing. Did you catch a cold?

熱があるし、セキも出るし。＿＿＿＿か？

netsu ga aru shi, seki mo deru shi. ＿＿＿＿ ka?

have a fever / have a cough too

Most Japanese wear face masks when they catch colds so they don't pass their germs on to others. People with hay fever also wear face masks to avoid inhaling pollen. In the winter and early spring you can see many people wearing masks.

❹ Whoops! I forgot the keys!

あっ！カギを＿＿＿＿！

a! kagi o ＿＿＿＿!

keys

❺ Oh, I've been working overtime for quite a while now and I'm tired.

ふうう、ずっと残業が続いているので＿＿＿＿。 casual style

fūu, zutto zangyō ga tsuzuite iru node ＿＿＿＿.

whew / for a long time / continues

❻ Things at home are bothering me.

家庭のことで ______。

katē no koto de ______.
home things

❼ Now I remember!

やっと ______!

yatto ______!
finally

❽ Ah, I'm thirsty! A draft beer, please!

ああ、______! 生ビールお願いします。

ā, ______! nama *beer* o-negai shimasu.
draft please (a polite request)

❾ Mr. A: Did you lose weight?

______か?

______ ka?

Mr. B: No, I gained some weight because of the stress at work.

ううん、ストレス太りです。

ūn, *stress*-butori desu.
gaining weight from stress

---

answers ❶ onaka ga sukimashita ❷ wakatta ❸ kaze o hikimashita ❹ wasuremashita ❺ tsukarete iru ❻ komatte imasu ❼ omoidashimashita ❽ nodo ga kawakimashita ❾ yasemashita

muzukashii desu ne ...

Mr. Pole

I called a client to make an appointment for our next meeting and asked her, **raishū no kinyōbi wa dō desu ka?** ("What about next Friday?") But she said, **ūn ... raishū no kinyōbi wa chotto muzukashii desu ne** ("Hmm, Friday is difficult for me"). I couldn't believe it! She's Japanese, but she thought "Friday" was difficult to understand? What's so difficult about Friday? So I changed the day and said, **soredewa, kondo no kayōbi wa?** ("Well, how about this coming Tuesday?") But again she says, **gomen-nasai, kayōbi mo chotto muzukashii desu ne ...** ("Sorry, but Tuesday is difficult, too"). Hey, I'm not a native speaker, but even I understand Tuesday! Is she pulling my leg?

The word **muzukashii** can be used in a lot of ways other than simply meaning "difficult." Basically what she was doing was making a gentle refusal. **muzukashii desu ne ...** ("I'm afraid that I can't ...") sounds polite and is useful because using that phrase means that you don't have to give a reason for the refusal.

Hirayama

using muzukashii to make gentle refusals

難しい

muzukashii

In Lesson 3 we learned that chotto is a soft way to refuse requests or give other negative responses. muzukashii is another. It is often used together with chotto, e.g., chotto… muzukashii desu.

using breath sounds to help convey the refusal

To sound as much like a native speaker as possible, sharply draw in your breath through your closed teeth for a moment before saying, ūn … chotto … (drawing out both of these words). Both the intake of breath and the drawn-out pronunciation will show that you are thinking about the question.

Hmm … well … (implies "no")

ううん…ちょっと…

ūn ... chotto ... inhaling sharply

Hmm … well … I'm afraid not …
(implying "no" or "I'm afraid it's not possible")

ううん…ちょっと難しいですね…。

ūn ... chotto muzukashii desu ne ... inhaling sharply

There are at least two different ways you can refuse using the phrase muzukashii: 1) to say simply chotto muzukashii, or 2) to give a reason and then say chotto … muzukashii.

REQUEST: Can you do it by tomorrow?

あしたまでにできますか？

ashita made ni dekimasu ka?
tomorrow by can you?

1) when you feel that a reason is not necessary:

(inhaling briefly) Hmm … well … I'm afraid not …
ううん…ちょっと難しいですね…。
ūn … chotto muzukashii desu ne …

2) when you feel that, for politeness' sake, a reason is necessary:

I don't have any time so, hmm, it's quite difficult…
時間がないのでちょっと…難しいですね…。
jikan ga nai node chotto… muzukashii desu ne …
time have none

OR

I don't have any time, so I can't do it.
時間がないのでできません。
jikan ga nai node dekimasen.
so cannot

(This is rather direct.)

muzukashii vs. taihen

complicated (antonym = easy): **難しい** muzukashii

Hmm … It's complicated! $\sqrt{2} \times \sqrt{5} \div 8 - 20$ …
難しいですね…。
muzukashii desu ne …

This problem is hard for me.
この問題は私には難しいです。
kono mondai wa watashi <u>ni wa</u> muzukashii desu.
this problem me for

We'd better stop talking about complicated issues.
もう難しい話はやめましょう。
mō <u>muzukashii hanashi</u> wa yamemashō.
now complicated issues let's stop

difficult (tough, hard, trying, terrible): **大変** taihen

It is <u>hard</u> to live in Japan because it is so expensive.

日本は物価が高くて大変です。

Nihon wa bukka ga takakute taihen desu.
prices high

Oh, how <u>terrible</u>!

大変ですね！

taihen desu ne!

That sounds like a difficult job [problem].

大変な仕事［問題］ですね。

taihen na shigoto [mondai] desu ne.
work

the kanji for muzukashii

難

nan/muzuka(shii)/kata(shi): difficult; hard; tough

One calamity follows on the heels of another. (a sea of troubles)

一難去ってまた一難

ichi-nan satte mata ichi-nan
one trouble leaves again one trouble

Easier said than done.

言うは易く行うは難し

iu wa yasuku okonau wa katashi
say easy do difficult (classical form)

There are black days ahead.

前途多難

zento-tanan
future full of troubles

PRACTICE

Fill in the blanks with the correct phrase from the list above, under "the kanji for muzukashii."

❶ The young employees don't even know how to greet people politely. I know there is trouble ahead for them.

新入社員はあいさつもできない。ふうう ______ だなあ。

shinnyū-shain wa aisatsu mo dekinai. fūu ______ da nā.
new employees greetings either can't do

❷ First my son failed his school entrance exam, and now my husband is out of work! It's been a sea of troubles.

息子が受験に失敗したら、今度は主人が失業、______ です。

musuko ga juken ni shippai shitara, kondo wa shujin ga
my son exam fail this time my husband

shitsugyō, ______ desu.
lose one's job

❸ It is not that easy! Easier said than done.

そう簡単にはできません！ ______ です。

sō kantan ni wa dekimasen! ______ desu.
so easy cannot

---

answers ❶ zento-tanan
❷ ichi-nan satte mata ichi-nan
❸ iu wa yasuku okonau wa katashi

JANGLISH

The following are phrases commonly used in conversation in Japan and believed by many Japanese people to be direct borrowings from English and other foreign languages. So when Japanese use these phrases in conversation with you, they may be confused when you do not understand. So it can be helpful to learn these "Japanese English," or Janglish, phrases!

Draw a line from the phrase at left that matches the meaning at right.

❶ ノータッチ *no touch*	(A) to be dismissed from one's job
❷ アメリカン *American*	(B) a young job-hopper
❸ ホット *hot*	(C) to be in love with each other
❹ オーエル *O.L.*	(D) to have nothing to do with
❺ ラブラブ *love love*	(E) a woman who works in an office; a clerk
❻ バージョンアップ *version up*	(F) a cup of hot coffee
❼ サラリーマン *salaryman*	(G) a behind-the-scenes worker who quietly supports and helps others
❽ フリーター *freeter*	(H) a period of being absent or taking a rest
❾ バック *back*	(I) a white-collar worker; a businessman
	(J) to always do and behave in the same way (in the same pattern)

❿ ブランク
blank

⓫ リストラ
restru(cturing)

⓬ ゴールイン
goal-in

⓭ インプット
input

⓮ ワンマン
one-man

⓯ ワンパターン
one-pattern

⓰ マイペース
my pace

⓱ ヴァージンロード
virgin road

(K) the (wedding) aisle

(L) a self-centered person who does as he likes, without listening to others

(M) to upgrade

(N) a cup of coffee that is weaker than regular coffee

(O) always operating at one's own speed, even if others around are moving faster

(P) to memorize; to learn by heart

(Q) to get married

answers ❶—D ❷—N ❸—F ❹—E ❺—C ❻—M ❼—I ❽—B ❾—G
❿—H ⓫—A ⓬—Q ⓭—P ⓮—L ⓯—J ⓰—O ⓱—K

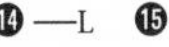

0141, **o i shi i** (delicious)

Mr. Pole

I've been studying the kanji numerals and that's been helpful, but recently I encountered a new problem with numbers. I asked a friend for the telephone number of a **yakiniku** (Korean barbecue) restaurant she had recommended. She gave me the name of the place and said, **koko wa ichiban oniku oishii** ("The most delicious meat is served here"). I asked her again for the number, and she said she'd just given it to me! We're going to the restaurant next week, but I haven't been able to call yet to make a reservation! What should I do?

Don't worry, Mr. Pole! Here's the number: 5501-0290. It's easy to figure out. Do you know how I did it? Japanese often use **goro-awase**, a form of punning or wordplay used to remember certain things like telephone numbers. A lot of businesses use **goro-awase** in their advertisements—with, for instance, phrases that describe their services—to help potential customers remember the telephone number.

Hirayama

each number has various pronunciations

0 (zero, rē, maru, o, wa)
1 (ichi, i, hitotsu, hi)
2 (ni, futatsu, fu)
3 (san, sa, mittsu, mi)
4 (shi, yottsu, yon, yo)
5 (go, ko, itsutsu, itsu)
6 (roku, ro, muttsu, mu)
7 (shichi, nana, nanatsu, na)
8 (hachi, ha, yattsu, ya)
9 (kyū, ku, kokonotsu, ko)
10 (jū, ju, tō, to)

PRACTICE

I. goro-awase with advertisements

Try to figure out the numbers hidden in the following ads. The romanized Japanese words in parentheses are not to be counted.

❶ (ad for a yakiniku steak house)

ko ko wa ichi(ban) ni ku oi(shii)
here No.1 meat delicious

("The meat served here is best")

❷ (ad for a temporary employment agency)

shi go to shi(nsetsu) na mi(na)san
work kind everybody

("Work for everyone who is kind")

❸ (ad for a moving service company)

go go wa i(tsumo) go ku rō san
afternoon always thanks for (your) hard work

("Afternoon always brings thanks for our help")

❹ (ad for a flower shop)

<u>ni ko ni ko</u> <u>ha na</u> wa <u>sa(kura)</u>
smiling flower cherry blossoms

("Smiles, flowers, cherry blossoms")

answers ❶ 5501-2901 ❷ 4510-4733 ❸ 5501-5963
❹ 2525-8703

II. goro-awase with dates

goro-awase is also used to refer to certain set dates in a playful way. Looking at the phrases below, can you guess what date (month and day) they refer to? (NOTE: The kanji for month is 月 [gatsu], and that for day is 日 [hi/nichi/ka].) For example, "letter day," or fumi no hi ふみの日, is 2月3日 [Feb. 3].

❶ mimi no hi _______
("ears day")

❷ niku no hi _______
("meat day")

❸ mushiba no hi _______
("cavity day")

❹ fūfu no hi _______
("couples' day")

❺ gomi-zero no hi _______
("no trash day")

answers ❶ 3月3日 (May 3) ❷ 2月9日 (Feb. 9) ❸ 6月4日 (June 4)
❹ 2月2日 (Feb. 2) ❺ 5月30日 (May 30)

kanji for units

In Lesson 5 you studied kanji numerals. There are also kanji for units such as hundred, thousand, etc.

10	100	1,000
十	百	千
jū	hyaku byaku	sen zen

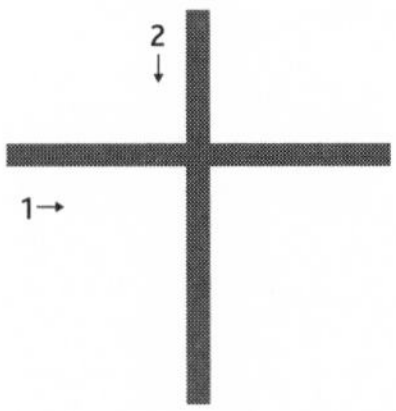

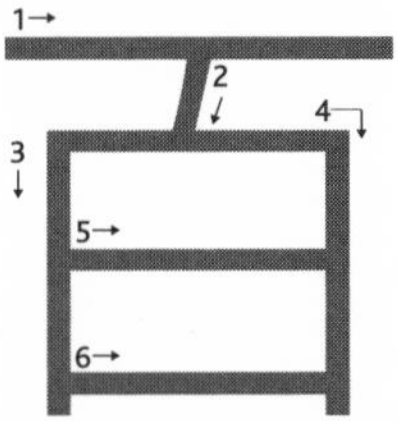

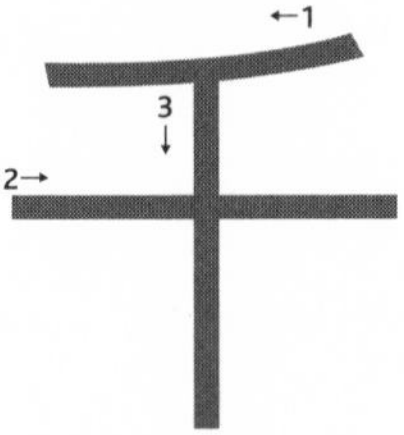

10,000	100 million	trillion
万	億	兆
man	oku	chō

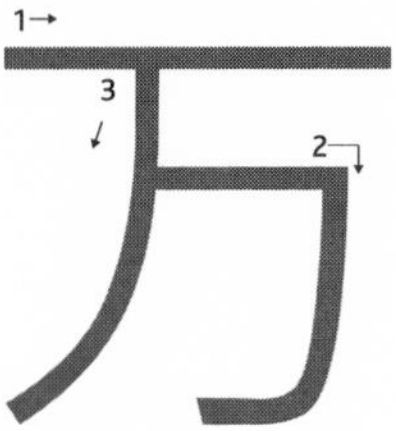

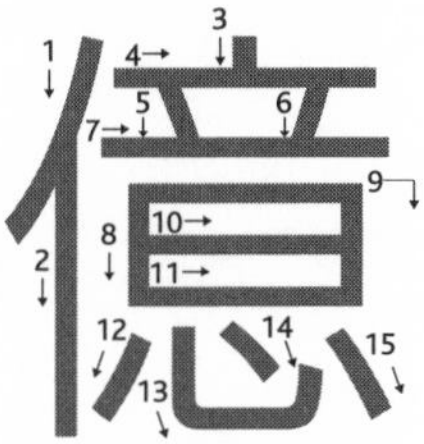

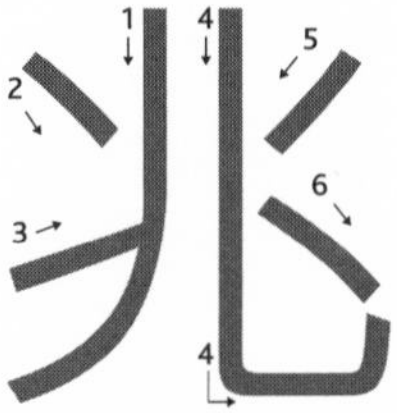

These kanji come in handy when dealing with Japanese yen. The kanji for yen (also seen in Lesson 5) is:

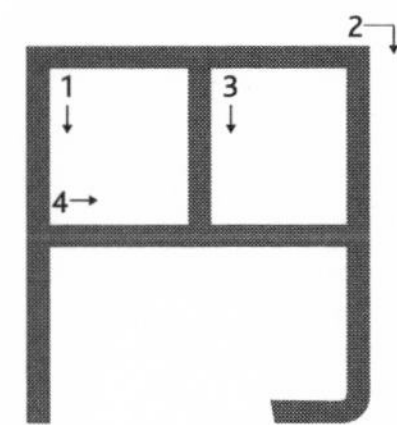

en (NOTE: not pronounced with a "y")

PRACTICE

Write the following amounts in kanji, followed by the kanji for yen.

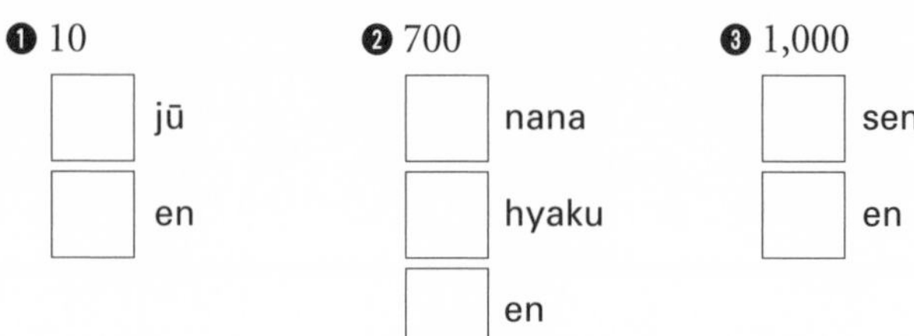

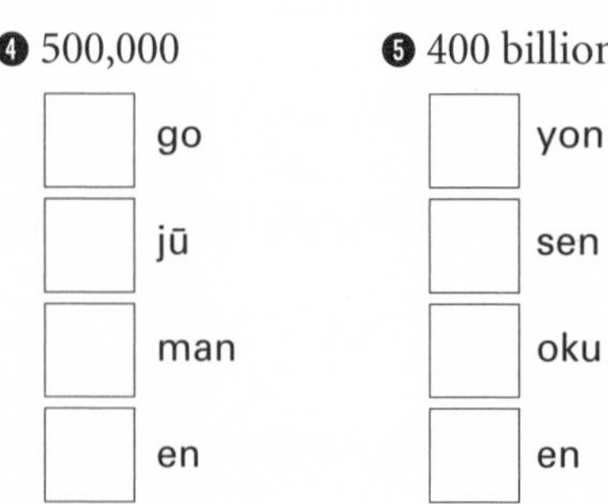

answers

❶ 十円

❷ 七百円

❸ 千円

❹ 五十万円

❺ 四千億円

numbers in newspapers

In Japanese newspapers, the numerals themselves are written as Arabic numerals, but they are paired with kanji for the various units like **hyaku** (hundred) or **sen** (thousand). (For example, 15,000 would be written 1万5千 **ichiman gosen.**) Write the following as they would appear in newspapers:

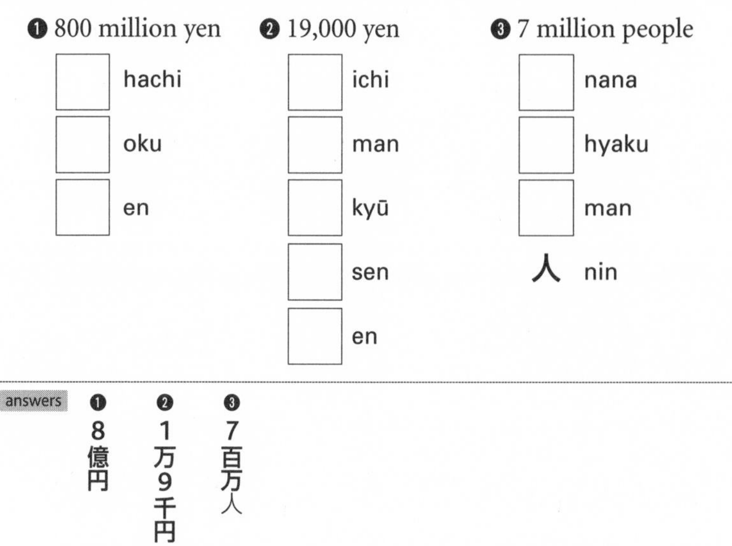

❶ 800 million yen
hachi
oku
en
❷ 19,000 yen
ichi
man
kyū
sen
en
❸ 7 million people
nana
hyaku
man
人 nin
answers
❶ 8億円
❷ 1万9千円
❸ 7百万人

phrases related to numbers

achieving success through family connections

（親の）七光り

(oya no) nanahikari
parents 7 lights

(Lit., "seven beams of parents")

most likely/ten to one

十中八九

jucchū-hakku
10 8 9

(Lit., "eight or nine of ten")

to get back on one's feet

七転び八起き

nanakorobi-yaoki
7 tumbles 8 get up

(Lit. "fall seven times, get up eight times")

PRACTICE

Fill in the blanks below with one of the phrases from above ("phrases related to numbers").

Don't feel so bad! You may fall many times in your life, but you can get back on your feet. Hang in there.

そんなにがっかりしないで ______ ですよ。がんばって下さい。

sonnani gakkari shinaide __❶__ desu yo. gambatte kudasai.
so much don't be disappointed you can do it

The company president's son found a good full-time job through his father's influences.

社長の 息子さんは ______ で就職しました。

shachō no musuko-san wa __❷__ de shūshoku shimashita.
president son got a job

Most likely, it is impossible.

______ 無理でしょう。

__❸__ muri deshō.
impossible probably

answers ❶ nanakorobi-yaoki ❷ (oya no) nanahikari ❸ jucchū-hakku

numbers considered unlucky in Japan: 4 and 9

In Japan, 4 and 9 are considered unlucky numbers. They have the same pronunciation, respectively, as "death" and "suffering," and are disliked for that reason. Automobile license plates, hospital floors and room numbers will often avoid the numbers 4 and 9. When giving flowers, candies, or other presents, avoid giving a set of 4 or 9 items. (It would be like giving someone 13 roses.)

4 shi	死 shi	死にます shinimasu to die
9 ku	苦 ku	苦しみます kurushimimasu suffer
		苦しい kurushii painful, agonizing
		苦労 kurō hardship

KANJI QUIZ

Each kanji is drawn with a certain number of separate lines, called strokes. When you want to look up a kanji in a dictionary without knowing its pronunciation, you can do it by counting the strokes.

EXAMPLES:

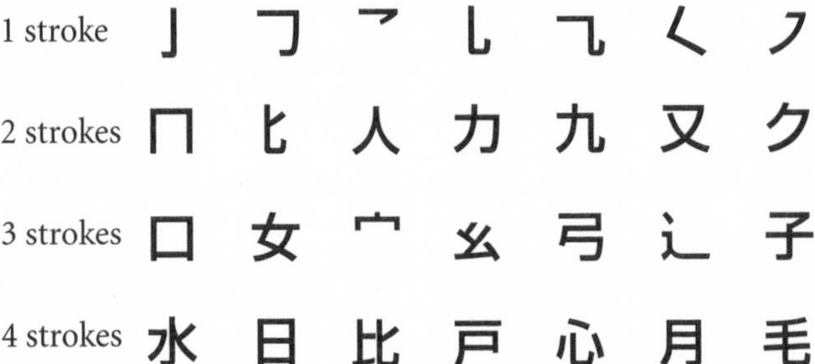

1 stroke
2 strokes 冂 匕 人 力 九 又 ク
3 strokes 口 女 宀 幺 弓 辶 子
4 strokes 水 日 比 戸 心 月 毛

NOTE: There are many more stroke patterns in Japanese than these.

I. 3-stroke kanji quiz

Find all the kanji in this block that are written with three strokes, and draw a vertical line through the middle of each one. When you finish, connect the lines to make a large three-stroke kanji.

中 乙 山 八 九
二 力 下 人 円
丸 七 口 日 川
久 手 子 今 大
夕 上 小 女 千

II. 4-stroke kanji quiz

Find all the kanji in this block that are written with four strokes, and draw a vertical line through the middle of each one. When you finish, connect the lines to make a large four-stroke kanji.

収	幻	厄	月	天	引	元
寸	田	世	戸	平	糸	申
生	立	本	今	氷	代	与
出	中	犬	少	木	日	本
夕	及	古	切	仕	用	凡
母	久	入	凶	刃	万	七
心	手	牛	反	火	円	公

answers

I.

中	乙	山	八	九
二	力	下	人	円
丸	七	口	日	川
久	手	子	今	大
夕	上	小	女	千

= 山 mountain

II.

収	幻	厄	月	天	引	元
寸	田	世	戸	平	糸	申
生	立	本	今	氷	代	与
出	中	犬	少	木	日	本
夕	及	古	切	仕	用	凡
母	久	入	凶	刃	万	七
心	手	牛	反	火	円	公

= 王 king

buri = "yellowtail"?

Mr. Pole

I thought **buri** was the name of a fish. I've learned in sushi restaurants that it means "yellowtail"! But lately I hear the word **buri** in news programs, and I know they're not talking about fish. They seem to be talking about time, like **ni-nen-buri** (2 years **buri**) or **yon-kagetsu-buri** (four months **buri**). Can you tell me what this -**buri** is, and how to use it?

Hirayama

This is the same **buri** used in the phrase **o-hisashiburi desu** ("Long time no see"). It's called an "emotional expression" because it's used to convey a feeling—in this case, a feeling of happiness or relief at doing something again after a long period. For example, if you said **senjitsu jūgo-nen-buri ni yūjin ni aimashita** ("The other day, I met a friend I hadn't seen in 15 years"), the implication would be that you were glad to see him or her again.

buri—an emotional expression

ぶり

buri is used to convey things like, "I was looking forward to … "; "I'm so happy to … "; "I really miss … "; "I've been waiting for …," etc.

To express that it has been a long, but unspecified, amount of time since you last did something, you can use hisashiburi.

I haven't (had something/done something) in a long time.
_______ は久しぶりです。
_______ wa hisashiburi desu.

I haven't had fish in a long time.
魚は久しぶりです。
sakana wa hisashiburi desu.

Long time no see.
お久しぶりです。
o-hisashiburi desu.

(The o- before hisashiburi is polite.)

If you want to state the length of time it's been, you can say, for instance:

It's been _______ since I've had/done _______.

_______ は _______ ぶりです。
(thing) (length of time)

I haven't eaten fish for 10 days.
魚は10日ぶりです。
sakana wa tōka-buri desu.

This phrase suggests that you are happy to have again something that you have been without for a while, so it is good to use if you are invited to a meal. Saying for instance, tempura wa hisashiburi desu will suggest your happiness to be having that dish.

expressing lengths of time

Lengths of time are expressed as follows:

hours	時間	jikan
weeks	週間	shūkan
months	ヶ月	kagetsu
years	年	nen

So, for example, 1 hour is ichi-jikan, 5 weeks is go-shūkan, 3 months is san-kagetsu, and 2 years is ni-nen. Be careful of the numbers 4 and 9; they are pronounced as follows (when speaking of lengths of time):

yo-jikan (4 hours)	ku-jikan (9 hours)
yon-shūkan (4 weeks)	kyū-shūkan (9 weeks)
yon-kagetsu (4 months)	kyū-kagetsu (9 months)
yo-nen (4 years)	kyū-nen (9 years)

Expressions used for numbers of days can also be confusing, so they need to be memorized.

1 day	1日	ichinichi
2 days	2日 (間)	futsuka (kan)
3 days	3日 (間)	mikka (kan)
4 days	4日 (間)	yokka (kan)
5 days	5日 (間)	itsuka (kan)
6 days	6日 (間)	muika (kan)
7 days	7日 (間)	nanoka (kan)
8 days	8日 (間)	yōka (kan)
9 days	9日 (間)	kokonoka (kan)

10 days	10日（間）	tōka (kan)
11 days	11日（間）	jūichi-nichi (kan)
14 days	14日（間）	jūyokka (kan)
20 days	20日（間）	hatsuka (kan)
24 days	24日（間）	nijūyokka (kan)

PRACTICE

Fill in the blanks below.

❶ Haven't seen you in a while!

_______ ですね。

_______ desu ne.

❷ It's been three years!

_______ ですね。

_______ desu ne.

❸ It's been ten years since I've driven a car.

車を運転するのは _______ です。

kuruma o unten suru no wa _______ desu.
(unten suru: drive)

❹ This is the first time in two months that it's rained.

雨が _______ に降りました。

ame ga _______ ni furimashita.
(furimashita: fall)

❺ I was busy, so I didn't come to the sports club for 3 weeks.

忙しかったのでスポーツクラブは _______ です。

isogashikatta node *sports club* wa _______ desu.
(isogashikatta: was busy; node: so)

❻ I wasn't feeling well so this will be my first time back at work in ten days.

具合が悪かったので会社に行くのは ______ です。

guai ga warukatta node kaisha ni iku no wa ______ desu.
was not feeling well so company will go

answers ❶ o-hisashiburi ❷ san-nen-buri ❸ jū-nen-buri ❹ ni-kagetsu-buri ❺ san-shūkan-buri ❻ tōka-buri

Lesson 17

capsule Japanese

Mr. Pole

I was talking with a friend the other day and she used the phrase **eco car**. I had no idea what she meant at first, but I figured out that it must mean "ecological car." My friend said Japanese people use that kind of abbreviated expression a lot. I liked it because it was interesting and catchy. Anyhow, do you know what "**eco car**" means, Hirayama-san?

You're right, it's short for "ecological car," or any type of environmentally friendly car. As your friend said, there are a lot of Japanese words that are shortened to make them quicker and easier to say. I call these terms "capsule Japanese." Many "capsule Japanese" words are condensed versions of English terms. (Often, the original English terms are rather lengthy and the shortened versions sound more like Japanese!) Capsule Japanese is casual.

Hirayama

capsule Japanese

Below are some examples of terms that are commonly shortened in Japanese. The syllables that are underlined make up the capsule version of the word. Try sounding them out.

❶ personal computer

パーソナルコンピューター

❷ remote control

リモートコントロール

❸ air conditioner

エアーコンディショナー

❹ convenience store

コンビニエンスストアー

❺ gaikoku-jin (foreigner)

がいこくじん

❻ gaikoku-sha (imported car)

がいこくしゃ

❼ Nippon ginkō (Bank of Japan)

日本銀行

(NOTE: The bank's name is Nippon Ginko, but the kanji 日 alone is pronounced "nichi.")

❽ car navigation system

カーナビゲーションシステム

❾ rental car

レンタルカー

❿ digital camera

デジタルカメラ

⓫ the [car] engine stalls/a stalled engine

エンジンストル

⓬ family restaurant

ファミリーレストラン

⓭ rusuban denwa (answering machine)

るすばんでんわ

⓮ dotamba *cancel* (last-minute cancellation)

ドタンバキャンセル

(dotamba: "at the last minute")

---

answers
❶ パソコン *pe(r)so(nal) com(puter)*
❷ リモコン *remo(te) con(trol)*
❸ エアコン *air con(ditioner)*
❹ コンビニ *conveni(ence store)*
❺ がいじん gai(koku)jin
❻ がいしゃ gai(koku)-sha
❼ 日銀 Nichigin(kō)
❽ カーナビ *car navi(gation system)*
❾ レンタカー *renta(l) car*
❿ デジカメ *digi(tal) came(ra)*
⓫ エンスト *en(gine) sta(lls)*
⓬ ファミレス *fami(ly) res(taurant)*
⓭ るすでん rusu(ban) den(wa)
⓮ ドタキャン dota(mba) *can(cellation)*

日本 Nihon? Nippon?

There are two ways to pronounce the kanji for Japan: **Nihon** and **Nippon**. The name **Nippon** is said to have been printed in Roman letters on ¥100 bills for the first time in 1885. The reason for writing the name that way on those bills was that the Minister of Finance and the head of the Bank of Japan were both originally from the area of Satsuma (now Kagoshima Prefecture), where that pronunciation was favored. Today Japan is usually called **Nihon**. **Nippon** is still used by some major companies, including the Bank of Japan (however, I've heard that the bank has recently started using "Nihon" as well). At international sporting events like the Olympics, most Japanese people root for athletes by saying **Gambare, Nippon**! ("Go, Japan!") but in ordinary contexts **Nippon** would generally be thought to sound old-fashioned.

PRACTICE

Mr. Pole is looking forward to his first date with a Japanese girl tomorrow. So, he went to Hakone the other day to check out places to visit on his big day. Fill in the capsule Japanese phrases in his story.

Hirayama: How did you like Hakone?

Mr. Pole: Well, I went in this **imported car** that I rented to drive there, but it **stalled** in the mountains, and the **air conditioning** broke down too. I found a nearby **convenience store**, but it was closed! I kept on walking and finally found a **family restaurant**.

______ を レンタルしたのですが… ______ して、
__❶__ o *rental* shita no desu ga … __❷__ shite,

______ も壊れてしまって…近くに ______ を
__❸__ mo kowarete shimatte (broke down) … chikaku ni (nearby) __❹__ o

見つけたけど、閉まっていました。少し歩いたらやっと

mitsuketa kedo shimatte imashita. sukoshi aruitara yatto
found but was closed a little finally

_______ を見つけました。

___❺___ o mitsukemashita.
found

When Mr. Pole finally got home, it was after 11 pm!

Then, I found a message from her on my **answering machine.** She'd **called off** the date **at the last minute**!

_______ にメッセージが入っていました。デートは _______ です。

___❻___ ni *message* ga haitte imashita. *date* wa ___❼___ desu.
was in

answers ❶ がいしゃ gaisha ❷ エンスト *ensta* ❸ エアコン *air con* ❹ コンビニ *conveni* ❺ ファミレス *fami res* ❻ るすでん rusuden ❼ ドタキャン dota *can*

more capsule Japanese

ピンからキリまで

pin kara kiri made
1 from 10 to

(This phrase that incorporates Portuguese terms means "from the best to the worst/a huge variety")

Often shortened to:

ピンキリ

pin-kiri

棚からぼた餅

tana kara botamochi
shelf from rice cake

(Lit., "a rice cake on a bookshelf," this phrase refers to a windfall/an unexpected piece of good luck)

Often shortened to:

たなぼた

tana-bota

TALK

Fill in the blanks below with one of the capsule phrases from above: pin kiri or tana bota.

Pole-san: I want to buy an old chest of drawers.

古いタンスを買いたいんです。

furui tansu o kaitai'n desu.
old chest want to buy

Any idea how much it will cost me?

いくらぐらいするか知っていますか？

ikura gurai suru ka shitte imasu ka?
about how much do you know?

Friend: Well, it depends on the chest—prices vary.

そうねえ、品物によって値段が ______ ですから。

sō nē, shinamono ni yotte nedan ga __❶__ desu kara.
goods depending on price

Speaking of chests, my uncle in the countryside has one. Shall I ask him (about prices)?

あ、そう言えば田舎のおじが持ってますよ。聞いてみましょうか？

a, sō ieba inaka no oji ga motte imasu yo. kīte mimashō ka?
countryside uncle has shal I ask?

Pole-san: By all means, please do.

ぜひお願いします。

zehi o-negai shimasu.
please

Friend: (The next day)
Pole-san, my uncle said he would give you the chest he has.

おじがポールさんにタンスをあげると言ってましたよ。

oji ga *Pole*-san ni tansu o ageru to itte mashita yo.
uncle give said to me I tell you

Pole-san: Really!?

うわあ、本当？

uwā, hontō?

Friend: Lucky you, Pole-san. (A chest has just landed in your lap.)

ポールさん ______ ですね！

Pole-san __❷__ desu ne!

---

answers ❶ pin-kiri ❷ tana-bota

JANGLISH QUIZ

The following are phrases commonly used in conversation in Japan that combine one element of Japanese and one element from a foreign language to make a word. So it's interesting and fun to learn these "Japanese English," or Janglish, phrases!

(Each definition in the list at left corresponds to a Janglish word formed from one element from the middle column and one from the right.)

❶ working flat out/at full power	1) 生 nama (raw)	A) メロ *melo(dy)*
❷ a draft beer	2) フル *full*	B) 金(融) kin(yū) (finance)
❸ friends made through e-mailing, or friends who communicate mainly through e-mails	3) 着 chaku (arrive)	C) ビール *beer*
❹ a full tank of gas	4) サラ *sala(ry)*	D) サラ *sala(ry)man*
❺ toothbrush	5) 歯 ha (teeth)	E) 友 tomo (friend)
❻ a mother who pushes her child too hard to excel in school	6) 顔 kao (face)	F) ブラシ *brush*
❼ taking advantage of the fact that your face is known, to get some special treatment (for instance, to get waved through a checkpoint)	7) 満 man (full)	G) タン *tan(k)*
❽ quitting a white-collar position to start one's own business	8) 教育 kyōiku (education)	H) パス *pass*
❾ the ringing of a cell phone that is set to play music	9) 脱 datsu (get out)	I) ママ *mama*
❿ moneylenders who allow individuals to borrow money without security, but with an extremely high interest rate	10) メル *mail*	J) 回転 kaiten (rotation)

answers

❶ 2—J **フル回転** *full* kaiten (working flat out)

❷ 1—C **生ビール** nama *beer* (draft beer)

❸ 10—E **メル友** *mail* tomo (friends through email)

❹ 7—G **満タン** man *tan(k)* (full tank)

❺ 5—F **歯ブラシ** ha *brush* (toothbrush)

❻ 8—I **教育ママ** kyōiku *mama* (mother who pushes her children to prove themselves in school)

❼ 6—H **顔パス** kao *pass* (free entry on sight)

❽ 9—D **脱サラ** datsu *sala(ry man)* (leaving the life of a businessman)

❾ 3—A **着メロ** chaku *melo(dy)* (ringing of cell phone set to music)

❿ 4—B **サラ金** *sala(ry)* kin(yū) (lenders of high-interest loans)

water words

Mr. Pole

Last month, I took my parents on a trip to Kyushu. The **onsen** (hot spring) was relaxing, the scenery was awesome, and the food was delicious! My friend Koga-san is from Fukuoka prefecture, so I told him about the trip. He said, **sō desu ka. oyako mizu-irazu deshita ne** ("I see. I guess there, was **mizu-irazu** ["no need of water"?] for your family"). He continued, **demo,** Pole-**san mizu-kusai desu ne** ("But, Mr. Pole, you are **mizu-kusai** ["stinking of water"?]). **Kyūshū nara iro-iro shōkai shitakatta desu** ("I would have liked to show you lots of places in Kyushu"). What did he mean?

What Mr. Koga meant is, "I guess you were happy to spend time alone with your parents. But Mr. Pole, I thought you were my friend! I could've taken you to a lot of good spots in Kyushu if you'd told me you were going." Japanese has many idioms that contain the word **mizu** (water). For example, **mizu shōbai**, which literally means "water business"—**mizu shōbai** is not the business of selling water! Its name suggests a trade that is as "liquid" and as changeable as water, and it refers to businesses that rely on remaining popular with customers, like bars, and nightclubs. In this chapter we'll have a look at a few expressions that use the word **mizu.**

Hirayama

phrases containing the kanji for "water"

mizu

suddenly unfriendly (toward a friend)/standoffish

水臭い

mizu-kusai
water smell

(Lit., "stinking of water")

to be alone with one's family, without outsiders

水入らず

mizu-irazu
water not letting in

(Lit., "no water enters"/"so close that no water can get in")

like oil and water

水と油

mizu to abura
water and oil

(Lit., "water and oil")

to forgive and forget

水に流す

mizu ni nagasu
water let flow

(Lit., "let flow away in water")

a drop in the bucket

焼け石に水

yakeishi ni mizu
burning stone water

(Lit., "water on a burning stone")

to come to nothing

水の泡

mizu no awa
water foam

(Lit., "foam on water")

a bolt from the blue (used about sudden bad news)

寝耳に水

nemimi ni mizu
sleeping ears water

(Lit., "water in a sleeping ear")

PRACTICE

Fill in the blanks with one of the phrases above.

❶ I was on a diet and I did great! But then I gained the weight back right away. All my efforts came to nothing.

がんばってダイエットしたのに、すぐに戻っちゃった。全てが ____ だった。

gambatte *diet* shita noni suguni modocchatta. subete ga _____ datta.
try hard soon went right back all

❷ Hey, I thought you were supposed to be my friend! I wish you had told me.

_______ なあ。遠慮しないで言ってくれればよかったのに！

_______ nā. enryo shinaide itte kurereba yokatta noni!
not hesitate if you had told me I with

❸ With this deficit, no matter how hard we try, it's only a drop in the bucket.

赤字なのでいくらがんばっても _______ です。

akaji nanode ikura gambatte mo _______ desu.
deficit no matter how much we try

❹ Those two are like oil and water. They're always fighting.

あの二人は ______。いつもけんかしている。

ano futari wa ______. itsumo <u>kenka shite iru</u>.
2 people / always / are fighting

❺ Oh, really? That's a bolt from the blue. I've never heard of it!

えっ、ホント？ ______。そんな事聞いてないよ！

e, honto? ______. sonna koto <u>kiite nai</u> yo.
really? / such / thing / not heard / I tell you

❻ Oh, what a relief! He told me he would forgive and forget. I'll be more careful in the future.

ああ良かった！ 今回の事は ______ と言ってくれました。これから気をつけます。

ā yokatta! konkai no koto wa ______ to <u>itte kuremashita</u>.
this time / matter / told me

kore-kara ki o tsukemasu.
from now / be careful

❼ We finally got to go away, just the two of us, to a hot spring, for the first time in ten years.

10年ぶりに夫婦 ______ で温泉に行った。

jūnen-buri ni fūfu ______ de onsen ni itta.
husband & wife / hot spring / went

polka dots
水玉模様
mizutama moyō
("droplet pattern")

---

answers ❶ mizu no awa ❷ mizu-kusai ❸ yakeishi ni mizu
❹ mizu to abura ❺ nemimi ni mizu ❻ mizu ni nagasu
❼ mizu-irazu

KANJI QUIZ

水

mizu/sui/zui: water

The kanji for mizu is used to form many different words. Here, select the kanji from the list on the facing page that, when combined with mizu, forms the word defined below.

❶ in the water
❷ waterproof
❸ runny nose
❹ seawater
❺ light blue
❻ athlete's foot
❼ perfume
❽ saving water
❾ public water
❿ water temperature
⓫ flood
⓬ rainwater

hana: nose

kō: fragrance

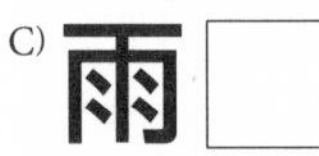
ama: rain

bō: defend; prevent

kai: sea

dō: road

on: temperature

chū: middle; inside

iro: color

mushi: insect

K) 節 □
setsu: moderate; restrain

L) 洪 □
kō: vast; flood

answers
❶ H) 水中 suichū
❷ D) 防水 bōsui
❸ A) 鼻水 hanamizu
❹ E) 海水 kaisui
❺ I) 水色 mizuiro
❻ J) 水虫 mizumushi
❼ B) 香水 kōsui
❽ K) 節水 sessui
❾ F) 水道 suidō
❿ G) 水温 suion
⓫ L) 洪水 kōzui
⓬ C) 雨水 amamizu

TALK

Taxi driver: So, where (what country) are you from?

お客さんはどこの国？ typical question from a taxi driver

o-kyakusan wa doko no kuni?
customer where country

Pole-san: I'm from the South Pole.

南極です。

Nankyoku desu.
South Pole

Taxi driver: What's your favorite Japanese food?

日本の食べ物は何が好き？

Nihon no tabemono wa nani ga suki?
food what like

Pole-san: Oh, I love fish!

魚が好きです。

sakana ga suki desu.
fish

Taxi driver: How do you like Japan?

日本はどう？

Nihon wa dō?
how?

Pole-san: I'm getting used to it.

少し慣れました。

sukoshi naremashita.
a little getting used to

Taxi driver: Do you have a family?

家族は？

kazoku wa?
family

Pole-san: I'm single.

独身です。

dokushin desu.
single

kūsha (empty)

Japanese taxis have digital displays in their windows that let you know if they are empty (**kūsha**; indicated by red characters) before you try to hail them.

hito no fundoshi de sumō o toru!?

= "doing sumo in someone else's underwear"?

Mr. Pole

One of my colleagues completed a successful project recently, so I told him, "Congratulations! You did a good job!" But some other colleagues who had helped him on the project came up to me and said, "Keep an eye on him, Mr. Pole! Because he is **hito no fundoshi de sumō o toru hito desu yo** ("doing sumo in someone else's **fundoshi**"?). I looked up **fundoshi** in a pocket-sized culture dictionary I'd brought when I first came to Japan. It said that it was an old-style loincloth made of a single long sheet of fabric, and that it was worn by men as underwear in the past. I couldn't believe that this guy was still wearing a **fundoshi**. I thought that sumo wrestlers wore something called **mawashi**, not **fundoshi**, correct? Ms. Hirayama, do Japanese men still wear **fundoshi**, even today?

I don't believe you can find anybody who actually wears **fundoshi** these days, (except perhaps at a festival) but I'm not sure. In any case, the phrase **hito no fundoshi de sumō o toru** actually means "benefitting oneself at someone else's expense." A similar phrase—that is a bit more polite since it doesn't mention **fundoshi**—is **tariki hongan** ("benefitting oneself with the help of others"). It's good to know about these two phrases, although of course they are disparaging and so you will want to use them with caution!

Hirayama

jo no kuchi—another sumo phrase

序の口

jo no kuchi

The rankings given to sumo wrestlers begin from jo no kuchi and go all the way to yokozuna (grand champion). jo no kuchi is the first rank, and it is also widely used in many situations to mean, "This is only the beginning." Therefore, it also implies, "Things are going to become harder and harder." Its meaning is further emphasized if you add mada ("yet") or honno ("just") before jo no kuchi—for mada jo no kuchi desu or honno jo no kuchi desu.

EXAMPLES:

Friend: Oh, my goodness! You've had a lot to drink!

うわあ、すごく飲みますね。

uwā, sugoku nomimasu ne.

really drink

Pole-san: Nah, nah. I've just gotten started!

いやいやほんの序の口ですよ。

iya-iya honno jo no kuchi desu yo.

no, no I tell you

Friend: Boy! This is heavy traffic!

ひどい渋滞ですね。

hidoi jūtai desu ne.

horrible traffic jam isn't it?

Pole-san: This is nothing. We haven't gotten to the peak yet.

まだまだ序の口ですよ。ピークはこれからですね。

mada mada jo no kuchi desu yo. *peak* wa korekara desu ne.

still from now

more idioms (not sumo-related)

The following are some comvenient idioms for business and daily life.

trial and error

試行錯誤

shikō-sakugo
test do confuse error

plans/ideas or opinions that may sound good on paper, but are not practical

机上の空論

kijō no kūron
desk empty discussion

(Lit., "empty discussion/theory on desk")

communication without words/tacit communication

以心伝心

ishin-denshin
by heart transmit heart

has both good points and bad points

一長一短

icchō-ittan
merits demerits

to be indecisive, hesitant

優柔不断

yūjū-fudan
flexible no decision

(Lit., "no decision, no conclusion")

constant rapid progress/constant evolution

日進月歩

nisshin-geppo
day advance month step

PRACTICE

Fill in the blanks with the idioms introduced above.

1. Friend: (receiving a phone call from Pole-san) Oh, Mr. Pole! I was just about to call you!

あ、ポールさん、今電話をしようと思っていました。

a, *Pole*-san, ima denwa o shiyō to omotte imashita.
now telephone was going to

Pole-san: I must have read your mind! (We can communicate even without words.)

_______ ですね。

_______ desu ne.

2. Pole-san: How is your new home?

新しい家はどうですか？

atarashii uchi wa dō desu ka?
new home how is?

Friend: It gets good sun, but it's far from the station.

日当たりはいいんですが、駅から遠いんです。

hiatari wa ii'n desu ga, eki kara toi'n desu.
sun good station far

Pole-san: So it has its good points and its bad.

_______ ですね。

_______ desu ne.

3. Friend: I bought my computer just last year, but there's already a newer version out.

コンピューターを去年買ったのにもう新しいバージョンが出たね。

computer o kyonen katta noni mō atarashii *version*
last year bought already new

ga deta ne.
came out

Pole-san: It's constant progress!

_______ ですね。

_______ desu ne.

❹ Friend: How's your new project coming along?

新しいプロジェクトはどう？

atarashii *project* wa dō?
how?

Pole-san: I'm working on it every day but I've still got a long way to go. It's a process of trial and error.

毎日がんばっていますが、まだまだ _______ です。

mainichi gambatte imasu ga, mada mada _______ desu.
(gambatte imasu: trying; mada mada: still)

❺ Friend: It always takes my brother forever to make a decision.

兄は何かを決める時はなかなか決められない。

ani wa nanika o kimeru toki wa nakanaka kimerarenai.
my brother something decide time never really decide

Pole-san: He sounds pretty wishy-washy.

_______ ですね。

_______ desu ne.

❻ Friend: I think that Ms. Kojima's ideas are good, but they never actually work.

小島さんのアイディアはいつも現実味がないね。

Kojima-san no *idea* wa itsumo genjitsumi ga nai ne.
reality-flavor

Pole-san: So they're only good on paper.

_______ ですね。

_______ desu ne.

---

answers ❶ ishin denshin ❷ icchō-ittan ❸ nisshin-geppo ❹ shikō-sakugo ❺ yūjū-fudan ❻ kijō no kūron

WORD GAME

Twelve words are hidden in this circle. How many can you find? (NOTE: Go clockwise.)

EXAMPLE:

きかい
kikai
machine

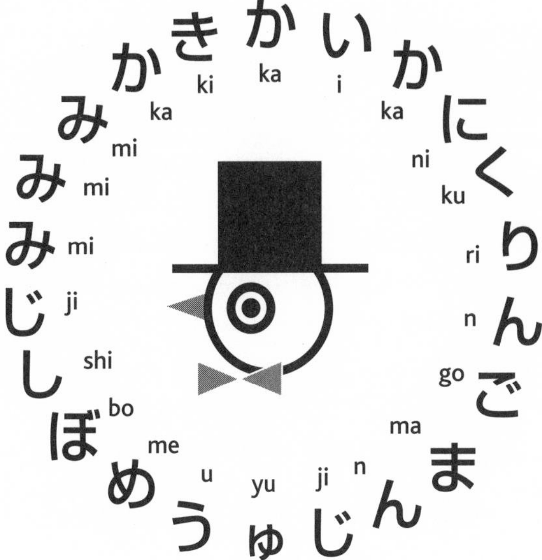

answers

きかい →	いか →	かに →	にく →	くり →	りんご →	ごま →
kikai	ika	kani	niku	kuri	ringo	goma
machine	squid	crab	meat	chestnut	apple	sesame

まんじゅう →	うめぼし →	しじみ →	みみ →	みみかき
manjū	umeboshi	shijimi	mimi	mimikaki
steamed bean-jam bun	pickled plum	type of shellfish	ear	ear pick

mahō no kotoba (magic words)

Mr. Pole

One of my colleagues was late to work the other day because she had a hangover. She said to me, **yūbe nomisugita kara chikoku shichatta**! ("I was late because I had too much to drink last night!") But to our boss she said, **yūbe nomisugita node chikoku shimashita**. Is there some difference between **kara** and **node** when explaining the reason for something?

When you want to explain the reason for something, you can choose **kara** or **node** (or sometimes **de**)—small but important words that convey different impressions to your listeners. **kara** is used more often in casual situations, and **node** in formal situations—business meetings, for example—and in writing. If you are unsure which word to use, remember it this way—use **kara** with your friends and **node** at work. (**de** has the same meaning as **node**, but is used in different types of sentences.)

Hirayama

expressing reasons or causes

から　ので　で

There are three words used to express reasons or causes:

reasons/causes	から kara / ので node / で de	result/conclusion

kara is used for emotional expressions. It can be used in friendly conversations to explain a personal reason or cause. But you should be careful how you use it because, depending on what you are talking about, using kara can sometimes make you sound selfish.

忙しかった	から	キャンセルをしました。
isogashikatta	kara	*cancel* o shimashita.
was busy		I canceled

I canceled it (the job) because I had another appointment (to meet a friend).

Even if the reason/cause is unreasonable, it starts to sound more logical if you use the magic words node and de!

node and de are used for giving logical reasons. (de is used with nouns.) These expressions are used in public situations and in polite speech. Public situations include business meetings and speeches. Logical reasons for something might be earthquakes or other natural phenomena, fire, accidents, illness, etc.

忙しかった	ので	キャンセルをしました。
isogashikatta	node	*cancel* o shimashita.
I was busy		I canceled

I canceled because I was busy (with work).

仕事	で	キャンセルをしました。
shigoto	de	*cancel* o shimashita.
work		I canceled

I canceled because of my work.

台風	で	キャンセルをしました。
taifū	de	<u>*cancel* o shimashita</u>.
typhoon		I canceled

I canceled because of the typhoon.

To compare, here is an example of the same sentence expressed three ways:

I was late because of a traffic jam.

渋滞だった**ので**遅くなりました。
jūtai datta **node** <u>osoku narimashita</u>.
became late

(sounds like it was not your fault)

渋滞**で**遅くなりました。
jūtai **de** <u>osoku narimashita</u>.
became late

(sounds like it was not your fault)

渋滞だった**から**遅くなりました。
jūtai datta **kara** <u>osoku narimashita</u>.
became late

(casual, used toward friends; sounds like you are making an excuse)

PRACTICE

Fill in the blanks with **kara**, **node**, or **de**, as appropriate.

■ to your boss

Could I go home, because I have a headache.

頭が痛い ______ 帰ってもいいですか？

atama ga itai ___❶___ kaette mo ii desu ka?
head painful may I go home?

■ casual, to a friend

I'm taking the day off tomorrow because a friend is coming over from France.

フランスから友達が来る ______ あした会社を休むよ。

France kara tomodachi ga kuru ___❷___ ashita kaisha o
from friend come tomorrow company

yasumu yo.
will take off I tell you

■ polite, to an acquaintance at work

I will be taking the day off tomorrow because a friend is coming from France.

フランスから友達が来ます ______ あした会社を休みます。

France kara tomodachi ga kimasu ___❸___ ashita kaisha o yasumimasu.

■ polite, to an acquaintance

I couldn't buy it because I didn't have any money.

お金がなかった ______ 買えませんでした。

o-kane ga nakatta ___❹___ kaemasen deshita.
money didn't have couldn't buy

■ **stating causes beyond your control**

The building collapsed because of the earthquake.

地震 ______ 建物はメチャクチャです。

jishin ❺ ______ tatemono wa mecha-kucha desu.
earthquake building destroyed

■ **to your friend**

I stayed home all day yesterday because it was raining.

きのうは雨だった ______ ずっと家にいました。

kinō wa ame datta ❻ ______ zutto uchi ni imashita.
yesterday was rain all day house was in

■ **stating causes beyond your control**

Many companies have gone bankrupt because of the recession.

不況 ______ 多くの会社が倒産しています。

fukyō ❼ ______ ōku no kaisha ga tōsan shite imasu.
recession many companies going bankrupt

■ **to your friend**

I had some time this afternoon, so I went to the gym. But I was really tired, so I just went in the sauna.

午後、時間があった ______ スポーツジムに行った。でもすごく疲れていた ______ サウナに入っただけだった。

gogo, jikan ga atta ❽ ______ *sports gym* ni itta. demo sugoku
afternoon time had went but really

tsukarete ita ❾ ______ *sauna* ni haitta dake datta.
was tired went in only

■ **polite, to a client**

It is because I am going on a business trip.

出張をします ______.

shucchō o shimasu ❿ ______.
business trip

■ **to your friend**

The movie I wanted to see was crowded, so I went to a different one. But I really do want to see that one after all, so I'm going to go tomorrow.

見たい映画が混んでいた ______ 他の映画を見た。でもやっぱりその映画が見たい ______ あした行こうと思う。

mitai ēga ga konde ita __⓫__ hoka no ēga o mita. demo
movie I want to see was crowded / another / watched but

yappari sono ēga ga mitai __⓬__ ashita ikō to omou.
after all / want to see / tomorrow / I think I will go

---

answers ❶ node ❷ kara ❸ node ❹ node ❺ de ❻ kara
❼ de ❽ kara ❾ kara ❿ node ⓫ kara ⓬ kara

talking about reasons or excuses

	sounds logical	sounds illogical
reason	理由 riyū	訳 wake
excuse	弁解 benkai to defend/explain something	言い訳 iiwake to make excuses for oneself; justify

PRACTICE

Fill in the blanks with the appropriate word from the chart on the preceding page.

❶ Stop making excuses! (illogical excuse)

_______ はやめなさい。

_______ wa yamenasai.
stop it

❷ I have no idea why it turned out like this. (illogical reason)

どうしてこうなったのか _______ がわからないです。

dōshite kō natta no ka _______ ga wakaranai desu.
why turned out this way don't know

❸ You'd better acknowledge your mistakes, instead of going on and on trying to defend them. (logical excuse)

ずっと _______ をするより素直に認めたほうがいいですよ。

zutto _______ o suru yori sunao ni mitometa hō ga ii desu yo.
for a long time straightforwardly had better acknowledge

❹ The more you make excuses, the more it sounds like you're lying! (illogical excuse)

_______ をすればするほど嘘に聞こえます。

_______ o sureba suru hodo uso ni kikoemasu.
the more you lie sounds

❺ Did he explain the reasons? (logical reason)

何か _______ を言ってましたか？

nanika _______ o itte mashita ka?
something said

❻ No matter how hard you try to rationalize this, it's too late! (logical excuse)

いくら _______ してももう遅いです。

ikura _______ shite mo mō osoi desu.
no matter how much already late

answers ❶ iiwake ❷ wake ❸ benkai ❹ iiwake ❺ riyū ❻ benkai

another magic word

ずっと　ずうっと　ずうーっと　ずうーーっと

zutto ⟶ zūuutto

zutto means "the whole time/for a long time/[something is] long." It can be used by itself to mean that something will continue for a long time (and is used with positive and negative meanings alike). People often stretch it out when saying it, zuuuuuutto, as if to underline the length of time that it suggests.

for a whole hour

一時間ずっと

ichi-jikan zutto

for a whole day

一日中ずうっと

ichinichijū zūtto

for a whole year

一年ずっと

ichi-nen zutto

for (my) whole life

一生ずうっと

isshō zūtto

これからもずうーーっと
日本語を勉強しましょうね！
korekara mo zūuutto
Nihongo o benkyō shimashō ne!
あ
い
う
お
え

Depending on how long it is stretched out, this one small word can express the speaker's feelings about a particular length of time, whether in the past or the future. For example:

Let's always keep on studying Japanese!

これからもずうっと日本語を勉強しましょうね!

korekara mo zūutto Nihongo o benkyō shimashō ne!
from now　　　　let's study

日本語をネイティブのように話す秘訣
Breakthrough Japanese

2004年9月24日　第1刷発行

著　者　平山ひとみ
発行者　畑野文夫
発行所　講談社インターナショナル株式会社
〒112-8652　東京都文京区音羽 1-17-14
電話　03-3944-6493（編集部）
03-3944-6492（営業部・業務部）
ホームページ　www.kodansha-intl.com

印刷・製本所　大日本印刷株式会社

定価はカバーに表示してあります。

ISBN4-7700-2873-3

JAPANESE LANGUAGE GUIDES

Easy-to-use guides to essential language skills

13 SECRETS FOR SPEAKING FLUENT JAPANESE

日本語をペラペラ話すための13の秘訣 *Giles Murray*

The most fun, rewarding, and universal techniques of successful learners of Japanese that anyone can put immediately to use. A unique and exciting alternative, full of lively commentaries, comical illustrations, and brain-teasing puzzles.

Paperback, 184 pages; ISBN 4-7700-2302-2

BREAKING INTO JAPANESE LITERATURE: Seven Modern Classics in Parallel Text

日本語を読むための七つの物語 *Giles Murray*

Read classics of modern Japanese fiction in the original with the aid of a built-in, customized dictionary, free MP3 sound files of professional Japanese narrators reading the stories, and literal English translations. Features Ryunosuke Akutagawa's "Rashomon" and other stories.

Paperback, 240 pages; ISBN 4-7700-2899-7

READ REAL JAPANESE: All You Need to Enjoy Eight Contemporary Writers

新装版 日本語で読もう *Janet Ashby*

Original Japanese essays by Yoko Mori, Ryuichi Sakamoto, Machi Tawara, Shoichi Nejime, Momoko Sakura, Seiko Ito, Banana Yoshimoto, and Haruki Murakami. With vocabulary lists giving the English for Japanese words and phrases and also notes on grammar, nuance, and idiomatic usage.

Paperback, 168 pages; ISBN 4-7700-2936-5

ALL ABOUT PARTICLES 新装版 助詞で変わるあなたの日本語 *Naoko Chino*

The most common and less common particles brought together and broken down into some 200 usages, with abundant sample sentences.

Paperback, 160 pages; ISBN 4-7700-2781-8

JAPANESE VERBS AT A GLANCE 新装版 日本語の動詞 *Naoko Chino*

Clear and straightforward explanations of Japanese verbs—their functions, forms, roles, and politeness levels.

Paperback, 180 pages; ISBN 4-7700-2765-6

THE HANDBOOK OF JAPANESE VERBS

日本語動詞ハンドブック *Taeko Kamiya*

An indispensable reference and guide to Japanese verbs aimed at beginning and intermediate students. Precisely the book that verb-challenged students have been looking for.

- Verbs are grouped, conjugated, and combined with auxiliaries
- Different forms are used in sentences
- Each form is followed by reinforcing examples and exercises

Paperback, 256 pages; ISBN 4-7700-2683-8

THE HANDBOOK OF JAPANESE ADJECTIVES AND ADVERBS

日本語形容詞・副詞ハンドブック *Taeko Kamiya*

The ultimate reference manual for those seeking a deeper understanding of Japanese adjectives and adverbs and how they are used in sentences. Ideal, too, for those simply wishing to expand their vocabulary or speak livelier Japanese.

Paperback , 336 pages; ISBN 4-7700-2879-2

www.kodansha-intl.com

JAPANESE LANGUAGE GUIDES

Easy-to-use guides to essential language skills

BEYOND POLITE JAPANESE: A Dictionary of Japanese Slang and Colloquialisms

新装版 役に立つ話しことば辞典 *Akihiko Yonekawa*

Expressions that all Japanese, but few foreigners, know and use every day. Sample sentences for every entry.

Paperback, 176 pages; ISBN 4-7700-2773-7

BUILDING WORD POWER IN JAPANESE: Using Kanji Prefixes and Suffixes

新装版 増えて使えるヴォキャブラリー *Timothy J. Vance*

Expand vocabulary and improve reading comprehension by modifying your existing lexicon.

Paperback, 128 pages; ISBN 4-7700-2799-0

HOW TO SOUND INTELLIGENT IN JAPANESE: A Vocabulary Builder

新装版 日本語の知的表現 *Charles De Wolf*

Lists, defines, and gives examples for the vocabulary necessary to engage in intelligent conversation in fields such as politics, art, literature, business, and science.

Paperback, 160 pages; ISBN 4-7700-2859-8

MAKING SENSE OF JAPANESE: What the Textbooks Don't Tell You

新装版 日本語の秘訣 *Jay Rubin*

"Brief, wittily written essays that gamely attempt to explain some of the more frustrating hurdles [of Japanese].... They can be read and enjoyed by students at any level." —*Asahi Evening News*

Paperback, 144 pages; ISBN 4-7700-2802-4

LOVE, HATE and Everything in Between: Expressing Emotions in Japanese

新装版 日本語の感情表現集 *Mamiko Murakami*

Includes more than 400 phrases that are useful when talking about personal experience and nuances of feeling.

Paperback, 176 pages; ISBN 4-7700-2803-2

BASIC CONNECTIONS: Making Your Japanese Flow

新装版 日本語の基礎ルール *Kakuko Shoji*

Explains how words and phrases dovetail, how clauses pair up with other clauses, how sentences come together to create harmonious paragraphs. The goal is to enable the student to speak both coherently and smoothly.

Paperback, 160 pages; ISBN 4-7700-2860-1

JAPANESE CORE WORDS AND PHRASES: Things You Can't Find in a Dictionary

新装版 辞書では解らない慣用表現 *Kakuko Shoji*

Some Japanese words and phrases, even though they lie at the core of the language, forever elude the student's grasp. This book brings these recalcitrants to bay.

Paperback, 144 pages; ISBN 4-7700-2774-5

A HANDBOOK OF COMMON JAPANESE PHRASES

日本語決まり文句辞典 *Sanseido*

Japanese is rich in common phrases perfect for any number and variety of occasions. This handbook lists some 600 of them and explains when, where, and how to use them, providing alternatives for slightly varied circumstances and revealing their underlying psychology.

Paperback, 320 pages; ISBN 4-7700-2798-2

www.kodansha-intl.com

JAPANESE SPIRITUALITY AND CULTURE

HAGAKURE The Book of the Samurai *Yamamoto Tsunetomo* 葉隠 山本常朝 著

Hagakure ("In the Shadow of Leaves") is a manual for the samurai classes consisting of a series of short anecdotes and reflections that give both insight and instruction in the philosophy and code of behavior that foster the true spirit of Bushido—the Way of the Warrior. As featured in the film *Ghost Dog*.

Hardcover, 192 pages; ISBN 4-7700-2916-0 Paperback, 184 pages; ISBN 4-7700-1106-7

THE BOOK OF FIVE RINGS *Miyamoto Musashi* 五輪書 宮本武蔵 著

Setting down his thoughts on swordplay, on winning, and on spirituality, legendary swordsman Miyamoto Musashi intended this modest work as a guide for his immediate disciples and future generations of samurai. He had little idea he was penning a masterpiece that would be eagerly devoured by people in all walks of life centuries after his death.

Hardcover, 160 pages; ISBN 4-7700-2801-6

MUSASHI An Epic Novel of the Samurai Era *Eiji Yoshikawa* 宮本武蔵 吉川英治 著

This classic work tells of the legendary samurai who was the greatest swordsman of all time.

"... a stirring saga ... one that will prove popular not only for readers interested in Japan but also for those who simply want a rousing read." —*The Washington Post*

Hardcover, 984 pages; ISBN 4-7700-1957-2

BUSHIDO The Soul of Japan *Inazo Nitobe* 武士道 新渡戸稲造 著

Written specifically for a Western audience in 1900 by Japan's under-secretary general to the League of Nations, *Bushido* explains concepts such as honor and loyalty within traditional Japanese ethics. The book is a classic, and as such throws a great deal of light on Japanese thinking and behavior, both past and present.

Hardcover , 160 pages; ISBN 4-7700-2731-1

THE UNFETTERED MIND Writings of the Zen Master to the Sword Master

Soho Takuan 不動智神妙録 沢庵宗彭 著

The philosophy and competitive strategy presented by the spiritual mentor to Musashi is as useful to today's corporate warriors as it was to 17th-century samurai.

Hardcover , 144 pages; ISBN 4-7700-2947-0 Paperback, 104 pages; ISBN 0-87011-851-X

THE BOOK OF TEA *Kakuzo Okakura* 茶の本 岡倉覚三 著

The seminal text on the meaning and practice of tea. Written 80 years ago, the book is less about tea than it is about the philosophical and aesthetic traditions basic to Japanese culture.

Paperback, 168 pages; ISBN 4-7700-1542-9

THE ANATOMY OF DEPENDENCE *Takeo Doi, M.D.* 甘えの構造 土居健郎 著

The classic analysis of *amae,* the indulging, passive love which supports an individual within a group, and a key concept in Japanese psychology.

"Profound insights not only into the character of Japan but into the nuances of dependency relationships." —*Ezra Vogel* **Paperback, 192 pages; ISBN 4-7700-2800-8**

THE ANATOMY OF SELF The Individual Versus Society *Takeo Doi, M.D.*

表と裏 土居健郎 著

A fascinating exploration of the role of the individual in Japan, and Japanese concepts of self-awareness, communication, and relationships. **Paperback, 176 pages; ISBN 4-7700-2779-6**

WORDS IN CONTEXT *Takao Suzuki* ことばと文化 鈴木孝夫 著

One of Japan's foremost linguists offers a provocative analysis of the complex relationship between language and culture, psychology and lifestyle.

Paperback, 192 pages; ISBN 4-7700-2780-X